Diabetics Desserts Cookbook

Unleash Your Sweet Tooth with Low-Sugar, Low-Carb Recipes for Healthier Indulgence

CARLY BLAIR

Warning-Disclaimer:

The purpose of this book is to educate and entertain. The author or publisher does not guarantee that anyone following the techniques, suggestions, tips, ideas, or strategies will become successful. The author and publisher shall have neither liability nor responsibility to anyone with respect to any loss or damage caused, or alleged to be caused, directly or indirectly, by the information contained in this book.

CONTENTS

INTRODUCTION..6

TIPS FOR MODIFYING TRADITIONAL DESSERT RECIPES.......................................7

CHAPTER 1: BAKING ESSENTIALS FOR DIABETICS 8

ESSENTIAL BAKING TIPS 9

CONVERSION CHART 10

CHAPTER 2: LOWCARB AND SUGARFREE TREATS 12

KETO BROWNIES 12
ALMOND FLOUR COOKIES 13
COCONUT FLOUR MUFFINS 14
SUGARFREE CHEESECAKE 15
LOWCARB LEMON BARS 16
KETO PEANUT BUTTER CUPS 17
SUGARFREE CHOCOLATE MOUSSE 17
ALMOND BUTTER FUDGE 18
COCONUT FLOUR BREAD 19
KETO CHAFFLE WAFFLES 20
LOWCARB PECAN PIE 20
KETO AVOCADO BROWNIES 21
SUGARFREE JELLO PARFAITS 22
KETO CHOCOLATE TRUFFLES 23
LOWCARB ZUCCHINI BREAD 24

CHAPTER 3: FRUITBASED DESSERTS 25

STRAWBERRY CHIA PUDDING 25
GRILLED PEACHES WITH HONEY YOGURT 25
RASPBERRY LEMON BARS 26
BAKED APPLES WITH CINNAMON 27
BLUEBERRY SMOOTHIE BOWLS 27
MIXED BERRY PARFAITS 28
MANGO SORBET 28
WATERMELON GRANITA 29
GRILLED PINEAPPLE WITH COCONUT CREAM 29
PINEAPPLE UPSIDEDOWN CAKE 30
RASPBERRY CHIA JAM 31
BLACKBERRY FOOL 31
CITRUS SALAD WITH HONEY 32
KIWI POPSICLES 32
STRAWBERRY RHUBARB CRISP 33

CHAPTER 4: DAIRYBASED DESSERTS 34

GREEK YOGURT PANNA COTTA 34

LOWCARB CHEESECAKE BITES..35

YOGURT BARK..36

RICOTTA CREAM WITH BERRIES..36

SUGARFREE RICE PUDDING..37

KETO CUSTARD TARTS..38

SUGARFREE RICE PUDDING..39

KETO CUSTARD TARTS..40

LOWCARB TIRAMISU...41

CHIA SEED PUDDING..42

KETO CREAM PUFFS...43

SUGARFREE PUMPKIN PIE...44

KETO CANNOLI..45

LOWCARB CRÈME BRÛLÉE...46

KETO CHOCOLATE MOUSSE CUPS..47

SUGARFREE FLAN...48

LOWCARB CHEESECAKE BARS..49

CHAPTER 5: DIABETICFRIENDLY CHOCOLATE DESSERTS 50

KETO CHOCOLATE CAKE...50

LOWCARB CHOCOLATE CHIP COOKIES...51

SUGARFREE CHOCOLATE TRUFFLES...52

KETO CHOCOLATE MOUSSE...53

SUGARFREE HOT CHOCOLATE...54

LOWCARB CHOCOLATE BROWNIES...55

KETO CHOCOLATE CUPCAKES...56

SUGARFREE CHOCOLATE PUDDING..57

LOWCARB CHOCOLATE TART...58

KETO CHOCOLATE LAVA CAKES..59

SUGARFREE CHOCOLATE MILKSHAKE..60

LOWCARB CHOCOLATE CREAM PIE...61

KETO CHOCOLATE BISCOTTI...62

SUGARFREE CHOCOLATE FONDUE..63

LOWCARB CHOCOLATE HAZELNUT COOKIES..64

CHAPTER 6: NUTTY AND SEEDY DESSERTS 65

ALMOND FLOUR COOKIES..65

PECAN SANDIES..66

KETO PEANUT BUTTER CUPS..67

CHIA SEED PUDDING..68

LOWCARB BAKLAVA..69

KETO PECAN PIE BARS...70

SUGARFREE HAZELNUT SPREAD...71

CASHEW BUTTER FUDGE...72

LOWCARB PISTACHIO BRITTLE..73

KETO WALNUT BROWNIES...74

SUGARFREE MACADAMIA NUT COOKIES..75

ALMOND FLOUR CAKE..76

LOWCARB PEANUT BUTTER CUPS..77

KETO SEED CRACKERS 78
SUGARFREE ALMOND BARK 79

CHAPTER 7: DIABETICFRIENDLY FROZEN DESSERTS 80

KETO ICE CREAM 80
LOWCARB POPSICLES 81
SUGARFREE FROZEN YOGURT 81
KETO MILKSHAKES 82
LOWCARB SORBET 82
SUGARFREE FROSTY 83
KETO ICE CREAM SANDWICHES 83
FROZEN CHEESECAKE 84
SUGARFREE FROZEN CUSTARD 85
KETO FROZEN YOGURT BITES 86
LOWCARB FROZEN FRUIT BARS 86
SUGARFREE FROZEN HOT CHOCOLATE 87
KETO FROZEN MOUSSE 87
LOWCARB FROZEN LEMONADE 88
SUGARFREE FROZEN PIE 88

CHAPTER 8: GLUTENFREE AND DIABETICFRIENDLY DESSERTS 89

COCONUT FLOUR BROWNIES 89
ALMOND FLOUR CUPCAKES 90
KETO LEMON BARS 91
LOWCARB MACAROONS 92
GLUTENFREE CHEESECAKE 93
KETO COCONUT CREAM PIE 94
LOWCARB MERINGUE COOKIES 95
SUGARFREE COCONUT PANNA COTTA 96
KETO ALMOND FLOUR CAKE 97
LOWCARB COCONUT CHIA PUDDING 98
GLUTENFREE KETO BREAD PUDDING 99
SUGARFREE COCONUT MACAROONS 100
LOWCARB ALMOND FLOUR COOKIES 101
KETO COCONUT CREAM PARFAITS 102
GLUTENFREE KETO BISCOTTI 103

CHAPTER 9: DIABETICFRIENDLY VEGAN DESSERTS 104

VEGAN KETO BROWNIES 104
CHIA SEED PUDDING 105
VEGAN AVOCADO CHOCOLATE MOUSSE 105
COCONUT MILK ICE CREAM 106
LOWCARB VEGAN CHEESECAKE 107
SUGARFREE VEGAN TRUFFLES 108
KETO VEGAN COCONUT MACAROONS 109
LOWCARB VEGAN CARAMEL SAUCE 110
VEGAN KETO PEANUT BUTTER CUPS 111
SUGARFREE VEGAN FUDGE 112

KETO VEGAN BREAD PUDDING..113
LOWCARB VEGAN FRUIT TARTS..114
VEGAN KETO CREAM PUFFS..115
SUGARFREE VEGAN PUMPKIN PIE..116
LOWCARB VEGAN COCONUT BARS...117

CHAPTER 10: DIABETICFRIENDLY HOLIDAY DESSERTS 118

FESTIVE LOWCARB PUMPKIN PIE..118
KETO PECAN PIE BARS 119
SUGARFREE GINGERBREAD COOKIES...120
LOWCARB YULE LOG 121
KETO EGGNOG CHEESECAKE..122
SUGARFREE CRANBERRY ORANGE BREAD..123
LOWCARB SHORTBREAD COOKIES...124
KETO PEPPERMINT BARK 125
SUGARFREE HOT CHOCOLATE BOMBS...126
LOWCARB FRUITCAKE 127
KETO GINGERBREAD HOUSE...128
SUGARFREE TRIFLE 129
LOWCARB BÛCHE DE NOËL...130
KETO MULLED WINE 131
SUGARFREE CHRISTMAS PUDDING 132

CHAPTER 11: DIABETICFRIENDLY DESSERT SAUCES AND TOPPINGS 133

SUGARFREE CARAMEL SAUCE..133
LOWCARB CHOCOLATE GANACHE...133
KETO STRAWBERRY SAUCE..134
SUGARFREE LEMON CURD..134
LOWCARB WHIPPED CREAM...135
KETO PEANUT BUTTER SAUCE 135
SUGARFREE RASPBERRY COULIS 136
LOWCARB BUTTERSCOTCH SAUCE...136
KETO CREAM CHEESE FROSTING..137
SUGARFREE BLUEBERRY COMPOTE 137
LOWCARB MAPLE SYRUP..138
KETO CHOCOLATE AVOCADO MOUSSE...138
SUGARFREE CUSTARD SAUCE...139
LOWCARB COCONUT CREAM 139
KETO SALTED CARAMEL SAUCE..140

30 DAYS MEAL PLAN 141

CONCLUSION 143

INTRODUCTION

Living with diabetes doesn't mean you have to deprive yourself of the sweet pleasures in life. In fact, with some smart substitutions and mindful portions, desserts can absolutely still be a part of your diet. This cookbook is all about showing you how to satisfy your sweet tooth without spiking your blood sugar levels.

As someone who has been living with type 2 diabetes for over a decade now, I know firsthand how difficult it can be to navigate food choices, especially when it comes to desserts. Diabetes is a chronic condition where the body doesn't produce enough insulin or can't effectively use the insulin it produces. Insulin is a hormone that regulates blood sugar levels, so when it's not working properly, blood sugar can rise to dangerous levels.

High blood sugar levels over time can lead to serious complications like heart disease, nerve damage, kidney disease, and vision problems. That's why managing blood sugar through diet and lifestyle changes is so crucial for those with diabetes. Carbohydrates, which are found in sugary foods, starches, fruits, and vegetables, have the biggest impact on blood sugar levels. When you eat carbs, they are broken down into glucose (sugar) and enter the bloodstream.

For people with diabetes, the goal is to keep blood sugar levels as close to normal as possible. This means limiting carbs, especially sugary and starchy foods, and focusing on foods that are high in fiber, protein, and healthy fats. That's where this cookbook comes in – providing delicious dessert options that are low in carbs and use smart substitutions to minimize blood sugar spikes.

I'll be honest, when I was first diagnosed with diabetes, I thought I had to say goodbye to all my favorite desserts forever. I quickly learned that this kind of deprivation mindset was not only unrealistic but also unhealthy. Completely restricting yourself from the foods you enjoy can lead to feelings of deprivation, which often results in overindulging or giving up on your healthy eating goals altogether.

The key is moderation and making smart swaps. Desserts can absolutely still be a part of a diabetic diet, but they need to be carefully portioned and made with ingredients that won't cause a blood sugar roller coaster. That's where this cookbook comes in – providing delicious, diabetesfriendly dessert recipes that will satisfy your cravings without derailing your blood sugar management.

I've learned through personal experience that allowing myself to indulge in a small, portioned dessert not only keeps me sane but also makes it easier to stick to my overall healthy eating plan. When I know I can have a delicious lowcarb brownie or a sugarfree cheesecake bite after dinner, I'm much less likely to feel deprived and overindulge on foods that aren't so diabetesfriendly.

TIPS FOR MODIFYING TRADITIONAL DESSERT RECIPES

One of the biggest challenges when it comes to desserts and diabetes is that traditional recipes are often loaded with sugar, refined flour, and other high carb ingredients. But with a few smart swaps, you can turn almost any dessert into a diabetes friendly treat.

Here are some of my goto tips for modifying traditional dessert recipes:

Use alternative sweeteners: Instead of regular sugar, opt for natural low carb sweeteners like stevia, monk fruit, or erythritol. These won't spike your blood sugar like regular sugar does.

Replace refined flour: Ditch the allpurpose flour and use nutrient dense, low carb flours like almond flour, coconut flour, or chickpea flour. These are high in fiber and protein, which helps slow down the absorption of carbs.

Add healthy fats: Incorporating ingredients like avocado, nut butters, and coconut oil not only adds moisture and richness to baked goods but also helps keep you feeling fuller for longer.

Load up on fiber: Fibrous ingredients like nuts, seeds, and berries can help balance out the carbs in desserts and prevent blood sugar spikes.

Watch your portions: Even with diabetic friendly desserts, portion control is key. Stick to small, satisfying servings and pair your treat with a protein or healthy fat to help stabilize blood sugar.

Throughout this cookbook, you'll find countless recipes that put these tips into practice, resulting in decadent desserts that are low in carbs, rich in fiber and healthy fats, and perfectly suited for a diabetic diet.

I know firsthand how challenging it can be to find desserts that are both delicious and diabetes friendly. But with a little creativity and the right ingredients, you can absolutely indulge your sweet tooth without compromising your health. This cookbook is all about empowering you to take control of your diabetes while still enjoying the flavors and textures you love.

So let's dive in and explore the world of diabetic friendly desserts together. From rich chocolate treats to refreshing fruity delights and everything in between, you'll find a world of sweet satisfaction that won't send your blood sugar soaring. Dessert is back on the menu, my friends – let's enjoy every bite.

Baking diabetic friendly desserts may seem daunting at first, but with the right ingredients and techniques, it can be just as enjoyable and delicious as traditional baking. Throughout my journey with diabetes, I've learned that the key to successful diabetic baking lies in understanding how to choose the right ingredients, master essential techniques, and practice portion control. Let's dive into the baking essentials that will set you up for sweet success!

Choosing the Right Ingredients

One of the biggest hurdles when it comes to diabetic baking is finding suitable replacements for sugar and refined flours. But trust me, with a little knowledge and creativity, you can whip up treats that are just as delightful as their traditional counterparts.

Sugar Substitutes

Let's start with the elephant in the room – sugar. Regular white sugar is a big nono for diabetics as it can cause rapid spikes in blood sugar levels. But fear not, there are plenty of tasty and natural sugar substitutes that can be used in baking:

Stevia: Derived from the stevia plant, this zerocalorie sweetener is extremely sweet and doesn't impact blood sugar levels. It comes in both powdered and liquid forms.

Monk Fruit Sweetener: Made from the monk fruit, this natural sweetener is gaining popularity for its clean, sugarlike taste and minimal impact on blood sugar.

Erythritol: A type of sugar alcohol that is naturally found in fruits and fermented foods, erythritol has a similar sweetness to sugar but with a fraction of the carbs and calories.

Xylitol: Another sugar alcohol, xylitol has a very similar taste and texture to regular sugar, making it a great 1:1 substitute in baking recipes.

When using these sugar substitutes, remember that they often sweeten differently than regular sugar, so you may need to adjust the amounts to suit your taste preferences.

Alternative Flours

Traditional allpurpose flour is high in carbs and can wreak havoc on blood sugar levels. Thankfully, there are many delicious and nutrientdense alternative flours that work beautifully in diabetic baking:

Almond Flour: Made from finely ground almonds, this flour is low in carbs, high in fiber, and adds a rich, nutty flavor to baked goods.

Coconut Flour: With its high fiber content and natural sweetness, coconut flour is a fantastic option for diabetic baking. Just be warned – a little goes a long way!

Chickpea Flour: Also known as garbanzo bean flour, this protein packed flour adds a lovely nutty taste and tender texture to baked treats.

Oat Fiber: Although not a traditional flour, oat fiber is a fantastic source of soluble fiber that can help reduce the impact of carbs on blood sugar levels.

When baking with alternative flours, it's important to remember that they absorb liquids differently than regular flour, so you may need to adjust the liquid amounts in your recipes.

Baking Techniques and Equipment

Once you've stocked your pantry with the right ingredients, it's time to dive into the baking techniques that will help you create perfectly moist, flavorful, and diabetes friendly treats.

ESSENTIAL BAKING TIPS

Always measure ingredients precisely: Baking is a science, so precise measurements are crucial for successful results. Invest in a good set of measuring cups and spoons.

Don't overmix batters: Overmixing can lead to tough, dense baked goods. Mix just until the ingredients are combined.

Use room temperature ingredients: Having ingredients like eggs, butter, and milk at room temperature helps them incorporate more easily and create a better texture.

Let baked goods cool completely: I know it's tempting to dive right in, but letting baked goods cool completely prevents them from becoming gummy or falling apart.

Experiment with substitutions: Don't be afraid to play around with ingredient swaps – like using mashed bananas or applesauce instead of oil – to reduce fat and carbs.

Here are some tips for practicing portion control:

Use smaller baking pans or ramekins: This automatically creates builtin portion control! Mini muffin tins and small ramekins are perfect for individual servings.

Preportion batters or doughs: Instead of cutting bars or slicing cakes after baking, scoop batter or roll dough into preportioned servings before baking.

Keep serving sizes in mind: Most diabetic dessert recipes provide serving size suggestions, so be sure to stick to those portions.

Add protein or fiber: Pair your dessert with a protein or fiber source like nuts, nut butter, or Greek yogurt to help stabilize blood sugar.

Satisfy cravings with smaller portions: Instead of depriving yourself of dessert, have a small, reasonable portion that satisfies your sweet tooth without sabotaging your blood sugar levels.

Remember, living with diabetes is all about balance and moderation – and that applies to desserts, too! By choosing diabetic friendly ingredients, employing smart baking techniques, and practicing portion control, you can absolutely indulge in delicious sweet treats without compromising your health.

Now that you've got the baking essentials down, it's time to get creative in the kitchen! The recipes ahead will put all of these tips and techniques into practice, proving that desserts don't have to be off limits just because you have diabetes. Sweet satisfaction is just around the corner – let's bake!

CONVERSION CHART

WEIGHT AND VOLUME CONVERSIONS

Weight	Volume (US)	Metric
1 oz	2 tbsp	28 grams
1 lb	16 oz / 2 cups	454 grams / 0.45 kilograms
1 gram	0.035 oz	0.035 oz
100 grams	3.5 oz	3.5 oz
500 grams	17.6 oz / 1.1 lbs	17.6 oz / 1.1 lbs

VOLUME CONVERSIONS (US)

Volume (US)	Metric
1 tsp	5 ml
1 tbsp	15 ml
1/4 cup	60 ml
1/3 cup	80 ml
1/2 cup	120 ml
2/3 cup	160 ml
3/4 cup	180 ml
1 cup	240 ml
2 cups	480 ml
4 cups (1 quart)	960 ml
1 gallon	3.8 liters

TEMPERATURE CONVERSIONS

Fahrenheit (°F)	Celsius (°C)
32°F	0°C
50°F	10°C
100°F	37.8°C
150°F	65.5°C
200°F	93.3°C
250°F	121.1°C
300°F	148.9°C
350°F	176.7°C
400°F	204.4°C
450°F	232.2°C
500°F	260°C

MEASURING EQUIVALENTS

US	Metric
1 cup flour	120 grams
1 cup sugar	200 grams
1 cup brown sugar	220 grams
1 cup powdered sugar	120 grams
1 cup butter	227 grams (2 sticks)
1 tbsp flour	8 grams
1 tbsp sugar	12.5 grams
1 tbsp butter	14 grams

LIQUID INGREDIENT CONVERSIONS

US	Metric
1 tsp	5 ml
1 tbsp	15 ml
1/4 cup	60 ml
1/3 cup	80 ml
1/2 cup	120 ml
2/3 cup	160 ml
3/4 cup	180 ml
1 cup	240 ml

This conversion chart should be useful for making adjustments and substitutions in recipes to make them suitable for a diabetic-friendly diet.

KETO BROWNIES

Prep: 15 mins | Cook: 25 mins | Serves: 12

Ingredients:

- 1 cup almond flour (120g)
- 1/2 cup unsweetened cocoa powder (50g)
- 1/2 cup granulated erythritol (100g)
- 1/4 teaspoon salt (1.25g)
- 1/2 cup melted butter (113g)
- 2 large eggs
- 1 teaspoon vanilla extract (5ml)
- 1/4 cup chopped pecans (30g) (optional)

Instructions:

1. Preheat your oven to 350°F (175°C). Grease an 8x8 inch baking pan.
2. In a mixing bowl, combine almond flour, cocoa powder, erythritol, and salt.
3. Stir in melted butter, eggs, and vanilla extract until well combined.
4. Fold in chopped pecans if desired.
5. Pour the batter into the prepared pan and spread it evenly.
6. Bake for 2025 minutes until a toothpick inserted into the center comes out clean.
7. Let it cool before slicing into squares.
8. Enjoy your guiltfree keto brownies!

Nutritional Info (per serving): Calories: 120 | Fat: 10g | Carbs: 5g | Protein: 3g

ALMOND FLOUR COOKIES

Prep: 10 mins | Cook: 12 mins | Serves: 18 cookies

Ingredients:

- 2 cups almond flour (240g)
- 1/4 cup granulated erythritol (50g)
- 1/4 teaspoon baking soda (1.25g)
- 1/4 teaspoon salt (1.25g)
- 1/4 cup melted coconut oil (56g)
- 1 large egg
- 1 teaspoon vanilla extract (5ml)

Instructions:

1. Preheat your oven to 350°F (175°C). Line a baking sheet with parchment paper.
2. In a bowl, mix almond flour, erythritol, baking soda, and salt.
3. Stir in melted coconut oil, egg, and vanilla extract until dough forms.
4. Scoop dough and roll into balls. Place them on the baking sheet.
5. Flatten each ball with a fork or your palm.
6. Bake for 1012 minutes until edges are golden brown.
7. Let cool on the baking sheet for 5 minutes, then transfer to a wire rack to cool completely.
8. Enjoy these delightful almond flour cookies!

Nutritional Info (per serving): Calories: 90 | Fat: 8g | Carbs: 2g | Protein: 3g

Prep: 10 mins | Cook: 20 mins | Serves: 12 muffins

Ingredients:

- 3/4 cup coconut flour (90g)
- 1/2 cup granulated erythritol (100g)
- 1 teaspoon baking powder (5g)
- 1/4 teaspoon salt (1.25g)
- 1/2 cup melted coconut oil (113g)
- 6 large eggs
- 1/2 cup unsweetened almond milk (120ml)
- 1 teaspoon vanilla extract (5ml)

Instructions:

1. Preheat your oven to 350°F (175°C). Grease or line a muffin tin with liners.
2. In a mixing bowl, combine coconut flour, erythritol, baking powder, and salt.
3. Add melted coconut oil, eggs, almond milk, and vanilla extract. Mix until well combined.
4. Spoon the batter evenly into the muffin cups, filling each about 3/4 full.
5. Bake for 1820 minutes, or until a toothpick inserted into the center comes out clean.
6. Allow the muffins to cool in the pan for 5 minutes, then transfer to a wire rack to cool completely.
7. Serve and enjoy these fluffy coconut flour muffins!

Nutritional Info (per serving): Calories: 120 | Fat: 10g | Carbs: 4g | Protein: 4g

SUGARFREE CHEESECAKE

Prep: 20 mins | Cook: 1 hour | Chill: 4 hours | Serves: 8

Ingredients:

- 2 cups almond flour (240g)
- 1/4 cup granulated erythritol (50g)
- 1/2 teaspoon cinnamon (2.5g)
- 1/2 cup melted butter (113g)
- 16 oz cream cheese, softened (450g)
- 1/2 cup granulated erythritol (100g)
- 2 large eggs
- 1 teaspoon vanilla extract (5ml)
- 1/4 cup sour cream (60ml)

Instructions:

1. Preheat your oven to 325°F (160°C). Grease a 9inch springform pan.
2. In a bowl, mix almond flour, erythritol, cinnamon, and melted butter to form the crust.
3. Press the mixture into the bottom of the prepared pan evenly.
4. In another bowl, beat cream cheese, erythritol, eggs, and vanilla extract until smooth.
5. Add sour cream and mix until combined.
6. Pour the cream cheese mixture over the crust.
7. Smooth the top with a spatula.
8. Bake for 5060 minutes until the edges are set but the center is slightly jiggly.
9. Turn off the oven and let the cheesecake cool inside with the door slightly ajar.
10. Refrigerate for at least 4 hours or overnight.
11. Slice and serve chilled. Enjoy your sugarfree cheesecake!

Nutritional Info (per serving): Calories: 380 | Fat: 34g | Carbs: 7g | Protein: 10g

Prep: 15 mins | Cook: 35 mins | Chill: 2 hours | Serves: 12

Ingredients:

- 1 cup almond flour (120g)
- 1/4 cup granulated erythritol (50g)
- 1/4 teaspoon salt (1.25g)
- 1/4 cup melted butter (56g)
- 3 large eggs
- 1/2 cup fresh lemon juice (120ml)
- 1 tablespoon lemon zest (15g)
- 1/4 cup powdered erythritol (50g), for dusting

Instructions:

1. Preheat your oven to 350°F (175°C). Grease an 8x8 inch baking dish.
2. In a mixing bowl, combine almond flour, granulated erythritol, and salt.
3. Stir in melted butter until the mixture resembles coarse crumbs.
4. Press the mixture into the bottom of the prepared baking dish.
5. Bake the crust for 1215 minutes until lightly golden.
6. Meanwhile, in another bowl, whisk together eggs, lemon juice, and lemon zest.
7. Pour the lemon mixture over the baked crust.
8. Return to the oven and bake for an additional 20 minutes, or until the filling is set.
9. Let the bars cool completely, then refrigerate for at least 2 hours.
10. Once chilled, dust the top with powdered erythritol.
11. Cut into squares and serve these tangy lowcarb lemon bars!

Nutritional Info (per serving): Calories: 90 | Fat: 7g | Carbs: 3g | Protein: 3g

KETO PEANUT BUTTER CUPS

Prep: 15 mins | Cook: 0 mins | Chill: 30 mins | Serves: 12

Ingredients:

- 1/2 cup unsweetened peanut butter (120g)
- 2 tablespoons powdered erythritol (30g)
- 1/4 cup coconut oil, melted (56g)
- 1/2 cup sugarfree dark chocolate chips (90g)

Instructions:

1. In a microwavesafe bowl, mix peanut butter and powdered erythritol until smooth.
2. In another bowl, melt the coconut oil in the microwave.
3. Stir the melted coconut oil into the peanut butter mixture until well combined.
4. Line a mini muffin tin with paper liners.
5. Spoon a tablespoon of the peanut butter mixture into each liner, filling them halfway.
6. Place the muffin tin in the freezer for 10 minutes to firm up the peanut butter layer.
7. Meanwhile, melt the sugarfree chocolate chips in the microwave in 30second intervals, stirring in between until smooth.
8. Remove the muffin tin from the freezer and spoon a tablespoon of melted chocolate over the peanut butter layer in each cup.
9. Return the muffin tin to the freezer for another 20 minutes to set the chocolate.
10. Once set, remove the peanut butter cups from the liners and enjoy!

Nutritional Info (per serving): Calories: 110 | Fat: 10g | Carbs: 2g | Protein: 3g

SUGARFREE CHOCOLATE MOUSSE

Prep: 15 mins | Chill: 2 hours | Serves: 4

Ingredients:

- 1 cup heavy cream (240ml)
- 1/4 cup powdered erythritol (50g)
- 1/4 cup unsweetened cocoa powder (25g)
- 1 teaspoon vanilla extract (5ml)

Instructions:

1. In a mixing bowl, beat the heavy cream with an electric mixer until soft peaks form.
2. Add powdered erythritol, cocoa powder, and vanilla extract to the whipped cream.
3. Continue beating until stiff peaks form and the mixture is smooth and fluffy.
4. Taste and adjust sweetness if necessary by adding more powdered erythritol.
5. Spoon the chocolate mousse into serving glasses or bowls.
6. Cover and refrigerate for at least 2 hours, or until set.
7. Serve chilled and enjoy this decadent sugarfree chocolate mousse!

Nutritional Info (per serving): Calories: 220 | Fat: 22g | Carbs: 2g | Protein: 2g

ALMOND BUTTER FUDGE

Prep: 10 mins | Chill: 2 hours | Serves: 16 squares

Ingredients:

- 1 cup almond butter (240g)
- 1/4 cup coconut oil, melted (56g)
- 1/4 cup powdered erythritol (50g)
- 1 teaspoon vanilla extract (5ml)
- Pinch of salt

Instructions:

1. In a microwavesafe bowl, mix almond butter, melted coconut oil, powdered erythritol, vanilla extract, and a pinch of salt until smooth.
2. Pour the mixture into an 8x8 inch pan lined with parchment paper.
3. Smooth the top with a spatula.
4. Place the pan in the refrigerator and chill for at least 2 hours, or until firm.
5. Once firm, remove the fudge from the pan and cut it into squares.
6. Store in an airtight container in the refrigerator.
7. Enjoy this creamy almond butter fudge as a guiltfree treat!

Nutritional Info (per serving): Calories: 120 | Fat: 11g | Carbs: 3g | Protein: 3g

COCONUT FLOUR BREAD

Prep: 10 mins | Cook: 45 mins | Serves: 12 slices

Ingredients:

- 6 large eggs
- 1/2 cup coconut oil, melted (113g)
- 1/4 cup unsweetened almond milk (60ml)
- 1 teaspoon apple cider vinegar (5ml)
- 1 1/2 cups coconut flour (180g)
- 1 teaspoon baking powder (5g)
- 1/2 teaspoon salt (2.5g)

Instructions:

1. Preheat your oven to 350°F (175°C). Grease a loaf pan with coconut oil or line it with parchment paper.
2. In a large mixing bowl, whisk together eggs, melted coconut oil, almond milk, and apple cider vinegar.
3. In another bowl, sift together coconut flour, baking powder, and salt.
4. Gradually add the dry ingredients to the wet ingredients, mixing until well combined and no lumps remain.
5. Pour the batter into the prepared loaf pan and smooth the top with a spatula.
6. Bake for 40-45 minutes, or until the top is golden brown and a toothpick inserted into the center comes out clean.
7. Allow the bread to cool in the pan for 10 minutes, then transfer it to a wire rack to cool completely.
8. Slice and serve this delicious coconut flour bread!

Nutritional Info (per serving): Calories: 150 | Fat: 12g | Carbs: 5g | Protein: 5g

KETO CHAFFLE WAFFLES

Prep: 5 mins | Cook: 5 mins | Serves: 4 waffles
Ingredients:

- 2 large eggs
- 1/2 cup shredded mozzarella cheese (56g)
- 1 tablespoon coconut flour (8g)
- 1/2 teaspoon baking powder (2.5g)
- Cooking spray (for greasing waffle iron)

Instructions:

1. Preheat your waffle iron according to manufacturer instructions.
2. In a bowl, beat the eggs.
3. Stir in shredded mozzarella cheese, coconut flour, and baking powder until well combined.
4. Once the waffle iron is hot, lightly coat it with cooking spray.
5. Pour a quarter of the batter onto the center of the waffle iron.
6. Close the lid and cook for 35 minutes, or until the chaffle is golden brown and crispy.
7. Carefully remove the chaffle from the waffle iron and repeat with the remaining batter.
8. Serve the chaffles warm with your favorite toppings, such as sugarfree syrup or berries.

Nutritional Info (per serving): Calories: 130 | Fat: 9g | Carbs: 2g | Protein: 9g

LOWCARB PECAN PIE

Prep: 15 mins | Cook: 40 mins | Serves: 8
Ingredients:

- 1 prepared lowcarb pie crust (storebought or homemade)
- 1 cup pecan halves (120g)
- 3 large eggs
- 1/2 cup granulated erythritol (100g)
- 1/4 cup unsalted butter, melted (56g)
- 1/4 cup sugarfree maple syrup (60ml)
- 1 teaspoon vanilla extract (5ml) and Pinch of salt

Instructions:

1. Preheat your oven to 350°F (175°C).
2. Arrange pecan halves in the bottom of the prepared pie crust.
3. In a mixing bowl, whisk together eggs, erythritol, melted butter, sugarfree maple syrup, vanilla extract, and a pinch of salt until well combined.
4. Pour the mixture over the pecans in the pie crust.
5. Place the pie on a baking sheet and bake for 3540 minutes, or until the filling is set.
6. Allow the pie to cool completely before slicing and serving.
7. Enjoy a slice of this delicious lowcarb pecan pie!

Nutritional Info (per serving): Calories: 280 | Fat: 25g | Carbs: 6g | Protein: 6g

Prep: 15 mins | Cook: 25 mins | Serves: 12

Ingredients:

- 2 ripe avocados, mashed
- 1/2 cup unsweetened cocoa powder (50g)
- 1/2 cup granulated erythritol (100g)
- 2 large eggs
- 1 teaspoon vanilla extract (5ml)
- 1/4 cup almond flour (30g)
- 1/4 teaspoon baking soda (1.25g)
- Pinch of salt

Instructions:

1. Preheat your oven to 350°F (175°C). Grease or line an 8x8 inch baking pan.
2. In a mixing bowl, combine mashed avocados, cocoa powder, erythritol, eggs, and vanilla extract until smooth.
3. Add almond flour, baking soda, and a pinch of salt. Mix until well combined.
4. Pour the batter into the prepared baking pan and spread it evenly.
5. Bake for 2025 minutes, or until a toothpick inserted into the center comes out clean.
6. Let the brownies cool completely before slicing into squares.
7. Serve and enjoy these fudgy keto avocado brownies!

Nutritional Info (per serving): Calories: 120 | Fat: 10g | Carbs: 6g | Protein: 3g

Prep: 10 mins | Chill: 2 hours | Serves: 4

Ingredients:

- 1 (0.3 oz) package sugarfree flavored gelatin mix (8.5g)
- 1 cup boiling water (240ml)
- 1 cup cold water (240ml)
- 1 cup sugarfree whipped cream
- Fresh berries for garnish (optional)

Instructions:

1. In a heatproof bowl, dissolve the sugarfree gelatin mix in boiling water, stirring until completely dissolved.
2. Stir in cold water until well combined.
3. Refrigerate the gelatin mixture for about 12 hours, or until partially set.
4. Once the gelatin has thickened but is still slightly liquid, layer it with sugarfree whipped cream in serving glasses or bowls.
5. Repeat the layers until the glasses are filled, ending with a layer of whipped cream on top.
6. Chill the parfaits in the refrigerator for at least another hour to fully set.
7. Before serving, garnish with fresh berries if desired.
8. Enjoy these refreshing and guiltfree sugarfree jello parfaits!

Nutritional Info (per serving): Calories: 15 | Fat: 1g | Carbs: 1g | Protein: 0g

Prep: 20 mins | Chill: 1 hour | Serves: 12 truffles

Ingredients:

- 4 oz unsweetened baking chocolate, chopped (113g)
- 1/4 cup heavy cream (60ml)
- 2 tablespoons powdered erythritol (30g)
- 1/2 teaspoon vanilla extract (2.5ml)
- Unsweetened cocoa powder or shredded coconut for coating

Instructions:

1. In a microwavesafe bowl, combine the chopped unsweetened baking chocolate and heavy cream.
2. Microwave in 30second intervals, stirring in between, until the chocolate is completely melted and smooth.
3. Stir in powdered erythritol and vanilla extract until well combined.
4. Refrigerate the mixture for about 30 minutes to 1 hour, or until firm enough to handle.
5. Once the mixture is firm, use a spoon or small scoop to portion out truffles.
6. Roll each portion into a ball between your palms.
7. Roll the truffles in unsweetened cocoa powder or shredded coconut to coat.
8. Place the coated truffles on a baking sheet lined with parchment paper.
9. Refrigerate the truffles for another 30 minutes to set.
10. Serve and enjoy these decadent keto chocolate truffles as a guiltfree treat!

Nutritional Info (per serving): Calories: 70 | Fat: 7g | Carbs: 1g | Protein: 1g

LOWCARB ZUCCHINI BREAD

Prep: 15 mins | Cook: 50 mins | Serves: 12 slices

Ingredients:

- 2 cups grated zucchini (about 2 medium zucchinis) (300g)
- 3 large eggs
- 1/4 cup melted coconut oil (56g)
- 1/2 cup granulated erythritol (100g)
- 1 teaspoon vanilla extract (5ml)
- 1 1/2 cups almond flour (180g)
- 1 teaspoon baking powder (5g)
- 1/2 teaspoon baking soda (2.5g)
- 1 teaspoon ground cinnamon (2.5g)
- 1/4 teaspoon salt (1.25g)
- 1/2 cup chopped walnuts (optional) (60g)

Instructions:

1. Preheat your oven to 350°F (175°C). Grease or line a 9x5 inch loaf pan with parchment paper.
2. Place the grated zucchini in a clean kitchen towel and squeeze out excess moisture.
3. In a large mixing bowl, whisk together eggs, melted coconut oil, erythritol, and vanilla extract until well combined.
4. Add grated zucchini to the wet ingredients and mix until evenly distributed.
5. In another bowl, whisk together almond flour, baking powder, baking soda, cinnamon, and salt.
6. Gradually add the dry ingredients to the wet ingredients, stirring until just combined.
7. Fold in chopped walnuts if using.
8. Pour the batter into the prepared loaf pan and smooth the top with a spatula.
9. Bake for 4550 minutes, or until a toothpick inserted into the center comes out clean.
10. Allow the zucchini bread to cool in the pan for 10 minutes, then transfer it to a wire rack to cool completely before slicing.
11. Slice and serve this delicious lowcarb zucchini bread!

Nutritional Info (per serving): Calories: 180 | Fat: 15g | Carbs: 5g | Protein: 6g

STRAWBERRY CHIA PUDDING

Prep: 10 mins | Chill: 2 hours | Serves: 2

Ingredients:

- 1/2 cup fresh strawberries, mashed (75g)
- 1 cup unsweetened almond milk (240ml)
- 1/4 cup chia seeds (40g)
- 1 tablespoon honey or sugarfree sweetener (15ml)

Instructions:

1. In a bowl, mix mashed strawberries, almond milk, chia seeds, and honey.
2. Stir well to combine all ingredients thoroughly.
3. Cover the bowl and refrigerate for at least 2 hours or overnight.
4. After chilling, stir the mixture again to ensure even consistency.
5. Serve chilled and enjoy this delightful strawberry chia pudding!

Nutritional Info (per serving): Calories: 120 | Fat: 6g | Carbs: 12g | Protein: 4g

GRILLED PEACHES WITH HONEY YOGURT

Prep: 10 mins | Cook: 5 mins | Serves: 2

Ingredients:

- 2 ripe peaches, halved and pitted
- 1/2 cup Greek yogurt (120g)
- 2 tablespoons honey or sugarfree syrup (30ml)
- Fresh mint leaves for garnish (optional)

Instructions:

1. Preheat grill to mediumhigh heat.
2. Place peach halves on the grill, cut side down.
3. Grill for 23 minutes until grill marks appear.
4. Flip peaches and grill for an additional 23 minutes.
5. In a bowl, mix Greek yogurt with honey until smooth.
6. Serve grilled peaches with a dollop of honey yogurt.
7. Garnish with fresh mint leaves if desired.
8. Enjoy these delicious grilled peaches with honey yogurt!

Nutritional Info (per serving): Calories: 160 | Fat: 2g | Carbs: 35g | Protein: 6g

Prep: 15 mins | Cook: 35 mins | Chill: 2 hours | Serves: 9

Ingredients:

- 1 cup almond flour (120g)
- 1/4 cup powdered erythritol (50g)
- Zest of 1 lemon
- 1/4 cup unsalted butter, melted (56g)
- 2 large eggs
- 1/4 cup fresh lemon juice (60ml)
- 1 cup fresh raspberries (150g)

Instructions:

1. Preheat your oven to 350°F (175°C). Grease or line an 8x8 inch baking pan with parchment paper.
2. In a bowl, mix almond flour, powdered erythritol, lemon zest, and melted butter until well combined.
3. Press the mixture into the bottom of the prepared baking pan to form the crust.
4. Bake the crust for 1012 minutes, until lightly golden.
5. Meanwhile, in another bowl, whisk together eggs and lemon juice until smooth.
6. Gently fold in fresh raspberries.
7. Pour the raspberry mixture over the baked crust.
8. Return to the oven and bake for an additional 2025 minutes, or until the filling is set.
9. Allow the bars to cool completely in the pan, then refrigerate for at least 2 hours before slicing into squares.
10. Serve chilled and enjoy these tangy raspberry lemon bars!

Nutritional Info (per serving): Calories: 120 | Fat: 10g | Carbs: 5g | Protein: 4g

BAKED APPLES WITH CINNAMON

Prep: 10 mins | Cook: 30 mins | Serves: 4

Ingredients:

- 4 medium apples, cored
- 2 tablespoons unsalted butter, melted (28g)
- 2 tablespoons granulated erythritol (30g)
- 1 teaspoon ground cinnamon (2.5g)
- 1/4 cup chopped walnuts (optional) (30g)

Instructions:

1. Preheat your oven to 375°F (190°C).
2. Place cored apples in a baking dish.
3. In a small bowl, mix melted butter, erythritol, and cinnamon.
4. Spoon the mixture into the center of each apple.
5. If using, sprinkle chopped walnuts over the top.
6. Bake for 2530 minutes, or until apples are tender.
7. Serve warm and enjoy these cozy baked apples with cinnamon!

Nutritional Info (per serving): Calories: 160 | Fat: 8g | Carbs: 22g | Protein: 1g

BLUEBERRY SMOOTHIE BOWLS

Prep: 10 mins | Serves: 2

Ingredients:

- 1 cup frozen blueberries (150g)
- 1 ripe banana, frozen
- 1/2 cup Greek yogurt (120g)
- 1/4 cup almond milk (60ml)
- Toppings: fresh blueberries, sliced bananas, granola, honey (optional)

Instructions:

1. In a blender, combine frozen blueberries, frozen banana, Greek yogurt, and almond milk.
2. Blend until smooth and creamy, adding more almond milk if needed to reach desired consistency.
3. Pour the smoothie into bowls.
4. Top with fresh blueberries, sliced bananas, granola, and a drizzle of honey if desired.
5. Serve immediately and enjoy these refreshing blueberry smoothie bowls!

Nutritional Info (per serving): Calories: 180 | Fat: 2g | Carbs: 40g | Protein: 6g

MIXED BERRY PARFAITS

Prep: 10 mins | Serves: 2
Ingredients:

- 1 cup mixed berries (such as strawberries, blueberries, and raspberries) (150g)
- 1 cup Greek yogurt (240g)
- 1/4 cup granola (30g)
- 2 tablespoons chopped nuts (such as almonds or walnuts) (15g)
- Drizzle of honey or sugarfree syrup (optional)

Instructions:

1. In two serving glasses or bowls, layer Greek yogurt and mixed berries.
2. Sprinkle granola and chopped nuts over the berries.
3. Repeat the layers until the glasses are filled.
4. Drizzle honey or sugarfree syrup on top if desired.
5. Serve immediately and enjoy these refreshing mixed berry parfaits!

Nutritional Info (per serving): Calories: 220 | Fat: 8g | Carbs: 25g | Protein: 15g

MANGO SORBET

Prep: 10 mins | Chill: 4 hours | Serves: 4
Ingredients:

- 2 ripe mangoes, peeled and diced (about 2 cups) (300g)
- 1/4 cup water (60ml)
- 2 tablespoons lime juice (30ml)
- 2 tablespoons honey or sugarfree sweetener (30ml)

Instructions:

1. In a blender, combine diced mangoes, water, lime juice, and honey.
2. Blend until smooth and creamy.
3. Pour the mixture into a shallow dish and cover with plastic wrap.
4. Place in the freezer for at least 4 hours, or until firm.
5. Once firm, remove the sorbet from the freezer and let it sit at room temperature for 510 minutes to soften slightly.
6. Use a spoon or ice cream scoop to scoop the sorbet into bowls.
7. Serve immediately and enjoy this refreshing mango sorbet!

Nutritional Info (per serving): Calories: 90 | Fat: 0g | Carbs: 24g | Protein: 1g

WATERMELON GRANITA

Prep: 10 mins | Chill: 4 hours | Serves: 4

Ingredients:

- 4 cups cubed seedless watermelon (600g)
- 1/4 cup fresh lime juice (60ml)
- 2 tablespoons honey or sugarfree sweetener (30ml)
- Fresh mint leaves for garnish (optional)

Instructions:

1. In a blender, combine cubed watermelon, lime juice, and honey.
2. Blend until smooth.
3. Pour the mixture into a shallow dish and cover with plastic wrap.
4. Place in the freezer for 1 hour.
5. After 1 hour, use a fork to scrape the partially frozen mixture, breaking up any ice crystals.
6. Return the dish to the freezer and repeat the scraping process every 30 minutes for about 34 hours, or until the granita has a slushy texture.
7. Once fully frozen and slushy, scoop the watermelon granita into bowls.
8. Garnish with fresh mint leaves if desired.
9. Serve immediately and enjoy this light and refreshing watermelon granita!

Nutritional Info (per serving): Calories: 60 | Fat: 0g | Carbs: 16g | Protein: 1g

GRILLED PINEAPPLE WITH COCONUT CREAM

Prep: 10 mins | Cook: 6 mins | Serves: 4

Ingredients:

- 1 pineapple, peeled, cored, and cut into wedges
- 1/4 cup coconut cream (60ml)
- 1 tablespoon honey or sugarfree syrup (15ml)
- Shredded coconut for garnish (optional)

Instructions:

1. Preheat grill or grill pan over medium heat.
2. Grill pineapple wedges for 23 minutes on each side, until grill marks appear.
3. In a small bowl, mix coconut cream and honey until well combined.
4. Remove grilled pineapple from the grill and arrange on a serving platter.
5. Drizzle coconut cream mixture over the grilled pineapple.
6. Garnish with shredded coconut if desired.
7. Serve immediately and enjoy this tropical grilled pineapple with coconut cream!

Nutritional Info (per serving): Calories: 100 | Fat: 3g | Carbs: 21g | Protein: 1g

Prep: 15 mins | Cook: 30 mins | Serves: 8

Ingredients:

- 1 can (20 oz) pineapple slices in juice, drained (565g)
- 1/4 cup unsalted butter, melted (56g)
- 1/2 cup granulated erythritol (100g)
- 8 maraschino cherries
- 1 cup almond flour (120g)
- 1/4 cup coconut flour (30g)
- 1 teaspoon baking powder (5g)
- 1/4 teaspoon salt (1.25g)
- 1/2 cup unsweetened almond milk (120ml)
- 1/4 cup unsweetened applesauce (60g)
- 2 large eggs
- 1 teaspoon vanilla extract (5ml)

Instructions:

1. Preheat your oven to 350°F (175°C). Grease a 9inch round cake pan.
2. Arrange pineapple slices in the bottom of the cake pan. Place a maraschino cherry in the center of each pineapple slice.
3. In a small bowl, mix melted butter and half of the granulated erythritol. Pour over the pineapple slices.
4. In another bowl, whisk together almond flour, coconut flour, baking powder, and salt.
5. In a separate large bowl, beat together almond milk, applesauce, eggs, vanilla extract, and the remaining granulated erythritol.
6. Gradually add the dry ingredients to the wet ingredients, mixing until smooth.
7. Pour the batter over the pineapple slices in the cake pan.
8. Bake for 2530 minutes, or until a toothpick inserted into the center comes out clean.
9. Allow the cake to cool in the pan for 10 minutes, then invert onto a serving plate.
10. Serve warm and enjoy this classic pineapple upsidedown cake!

Nutritional Info (per serving): Calories: 190 | Fat: 14g | Carbs: 12g | Protein: 5g

RASPBERRY CHIA JAM

Prep: 5 mins | Cook: 10 mins | Chill: 1 hour | Serves: 8 (2 tablespoons per serving)

Ingredients:

- 2 cups fresh raspberries (300g)
- 2 tablespoons chia seeds (30g)
- 2 tablespoons water (30ml)
- 2 tablespoons honey or sugarfree sweetener (30ml)
- 1 tablespoon lemon juice (15ml)

Instructions:

1. In a saucepan, combine raspberries, water, and honey over medium heat.
2. Cook, stirring occasionally, until raspberries break down and mixture thickens slightly, about 57 minutes.
3. Mash the raspberries with a spoon or fork to desired consistency.
4. Stir in chia seeds and lemon juice.
5. Continue to cook for another 23 minutes, until the jam thickens.
6. Remove from heat and let the jam cool to room temperature.
7. Transfer the jam to a jar or container and refrigerate for at least 1 hour to allow it to set.
8. Spread this delicious raspberry chia jam on toast, pancakes, or use as a topping for yogurt or oatmeal.

Nutritional Info (per serving): Calories: 30 | Fat: 1g | Carbs: 5g | Protein: 1g

BLACKBERRY FOOL

Prep: 10 mins | Chill: 1 hour | Serves: 4

Ingredients:

- 2 cups fresh blackberries (300g)
- 2 tablespoons granulated erythritol (30g)
- 1 cup Greek yogurt (240g)
- 1/2 cup whipped cream (120ml)
- Fresh mint leaves for garnish (optional)

Instructions:

1. In a blender or food processor, puree blackberries with granulated erythritol until smooth.
2. In a bowl, mix blackberry puree with Greek yogurt until well combined.
3. Gently fold in whipped cream until incorporated.
4. Spoon the blackberry mixture into serving glasses or bowls.
5. Cover and refrigerate for at least 1 hour to allow the flavors to meld.
6. Before serving, garnish with fresh mint leaves if desired.
7. Serve chilled and enjoy this light and creamy blackberry fool!

Nutritional Info (per serving): Calories: 100 | Fat: 4g | Carbs: 14g | Protein: 6g

CITRUS SALAD WITH HONEY

Prep: 15 mins | Serves: 4
Ingredients:

- 2 oranges, peeled and segmented
- 2 grapefruits, peeled and segmented
- 1 lime, juiced
- 1 tablespoon honey or sugarfree syrup (15ml)
- Fresh mint leaves for garnish (optional)

Instructions:

1. In a large bowl, combine orange and grapefruit segments.
2. In a small bowl, whisk together lime juice and honey until well combined.
3. Pour the honeylime dressing over the citrus fruit and gently toss to coat.
4. Refrigerate the salad for at least 15 minutes to chill.
5. Before serving, garnish with fresh mint leaves if desired.
6. Serve chilled and enjoy this refreshing citrus salad!

Nutritional Info (per serving): Calories: 70 | Fat: 0g | Carbs: 18g | Protein: 1g

KIWI POPSICLES

Prep: 10 mins | Freeze: 4 hours | Serves: 6
Ingredients:

- 4 ripe kiwis, peeled and sliced
- 1/4 cup water (60ml)
- 2 tablespoons honey or sugarfree syrup (30ml)

Instructions:

1. In a blender, puree kiwi slices, water, and honey until smooth.
2. Pour the kiwi mixture into popsicle molds.
3. Insert popsicle sticks into the molds.
4. Freeze for at least 4 hours or until completely frozen.
5. To remove popsicles from molds, run them under warm water for a few seconds.
6. Serve immediately and enjoy these refreshing kiwi popsicles!

Nutritional Info (per serving): Calories: 40 | Fat: 0g | Carbs: 10g | Protein: 1g

Prep: 15 mins | Cook: 40 mins | Serves: 6

Ingredients:

- 2 cups sliced strawberries (300g)
- 2 cups sliced rhubarb (200g)
- 1/4 cup granulated erythritol (50g)
- 1 tablespoon lemon juice (15ml)
- 1/2 cup almond flour (60g)
- 1/4 cup rolled oats (20g)
- 1/4 cup chopped pecans or almonds (30g)
- 2 tablespoons coconut oil, melted (28g)
- 1 tablespoon honey or sugarfree syrup (15ml)
- 1/2 teaspoon ground cinnamon (1g)

Instructions:

1. Preheat your oven to 375°F (190°C). Grease a baking dish.
2. In a large bowl, combine sliced strawberries, sliced rhubarb, erythritol, and lemon juice. Toss to coat evenly.
3. In another bowl, mix almond flour, rolled oats, chopped nuts, melted coconut oil, honey, and ground cinnamon until crumbly.
4. Spread the fruit mixture evenly in the prepared baking dish.
5. Sprinkle the crumble mixture over the fruit.
6. Bake for 3540 minutes, or until the fruit is bubbling, and the topping is golden brown.
7. Allow the crisp to cool slightly before serving.
8. Serve warm and enjoy this irresistible strawberry rhubarb crisp!

Nutritional Info (per serving): Calories: 180 | Fat: 10g | Carbs: 20g | Protein: 3g

GREEK YOGURT PANNA COTTA

Prep: 10 mins | Chill: 4 hours | Serves: 4

Ingredients:

- 1 cup plain Greek yogurt (240g)
- 1 cup unsweetened almond milk (240ml)
- 1/4 cup granulated erythritol (50g)
- 1 teaspoon vanilla extract (5ml)
- 1 packet (2 1/4 teaspoons) unflavored gelatin (7g)
- Fresh berries for garnish (optional)

Instructions:

1. In a small saucepan, pour almond milk and sprinkle gelatin over it. Let it sit for 5 minutes to bloom.
2. Place the saucepan over low heat and stir until gelatin dissolves completely.
3. In a mixing bowl, whisk together Greek yogurt, erythritol, and vanilla extract until smooth.
4. Gradually pour the warm almond milk mixture into the yogurt mixture, whisking continuously.
5. Divide the mixture evenly among four serving cups or ramekins.
6. Cover each cup with plastic wrap and refrigerate for at least 4 hours or until set.
7. Before serving, garnish with fresh berries if desired.
8. Enjoy this creamy and indulgent Greek yogurt panna cotta!

Nutritional Info (per serving): Calories: 90 | Fat: 2g | Carbs: 5g | Protein: 12g

Prep: 20 mins | Chill: 4 hours | Serves: 12 bites

Ingredients:

- 1 cup almond flour (120g)
- 2 tablespoons powdered erythritol (30g)
- 3 tablespoons unsalted butter, melted (42g)
- 8 oz cream cheese, softened (225g)
- 1/4 cup powdered erythritol (50g)
- 1 teaspoon vanilla extract (5ml)
- 1 large egg
- Fresh berries for topping (optional)

Instructions:

1. Preheat the oven to 325°F (160°C). Line a mini muffin tin with paper liners.
2. In a bowl, combine almond flour, 2 tablespoons powdered erythritol, and melted butter. Mix until crumbly.
3. Press the almond flour mixture firmly into the bottom of each muffin cup.
4. In a separate bowl, beat cream cheese, 1/4 cup powdered erythritol, and vanilla extract until smooth.
5. Add the egg and beat until well combined.
6. Spoon the cream cheese mixture over the almond flour crusts in the muffin tin, filling each cup almost to the top.
7. Bake for 2025 minutes, or until the cheesecake bites are set and slightly golden.
8. Allow the cheesecake bites to cool in the tin, then refrigerate for at least 4 hours to firm up.
9. Before serving, top each cheesecake bite with fresh berries if desired.
10. Enjoy these delightful lowcarb cheesecake bites!

Nutritional Info (per serving): Calories: 120 | Fat: 11g | Carbs: 2g | Protein: 3g

YOGURT BARK

Prep: 10 mins | Freeze: 4 hours | Serves: 4

Ingredients:

- 2 cups plain Greek yogurt (480g)
- 2 tablespoons powdered erythritol (30g)
- 1 teaspoon vanilla extract (5ml)
- 1/2 cup mixed berries, chopped (75g)
- 2 tablespoons unsweetened shredded coconut (15g)

Instructions:

- In a mixing bowl, combine Greek yogurt, powdered erythritol, and vanilla extract. Mix until smooth.
- Line a baking sheet with parchment paper.
- Spread the yogurt mixture evenly onto the parchment paper, about 1/4 inch thick.
- Sprinkle chopped mixed berries and shredded coconut over the yogurt.
- Place the baking sheet in the freezer and freeze for at least 4 hours or until firm.
- Once frozen, break the yogurt bark into pieces.
- Serve immediately as a refreshing treat!
- Store any leftovers in an airtight container in the freezer.

Nutritional Info (per serving): Calories: 90 | Fat: 4g | Carbs: 5g | Protein: 7g

RICOTTA CREAM WITH BERRIES

Prep: 10 mins | Serves: 2

Ingredients:

- 1 cup ricotta cheese (250g)
- 2 tablespoons powdered erythritol (30g)
- 1 teaspoon vanilla extract (5ml)
- 1 cup mixed berries (150g)
- Fresh mint leaves for garnish (optional)

Instructions:

1. In a mixing bowl, combine ricotta cheese, powdered erythritol, and vanilla extract. Stir until well combined and smooth.
2. Divide the ricotta mixture into serving bowls.
3. Top each bowl with mixed berries.
4. Garnish with fresh mint leaves if desired.
5. Serve immediately and enjoy this creamy ricotta cream with berries!

Nutritional Info (per serving): Calories: 200 | Fat: 12g | Carbs: 10g | Protein: 14g

Prep: 5 mins | Cook: 30 mins | Serves: 4

Ingredients:

- 1/2 cup Arborio rice (100g)
- 2 cups unsweetened almond milk (480ml)
- 2 tablespoons powdered erythritol (30g)
- 1 teaspoon vanilla extract (5ml)
- 1/4 teaspoon ground cinnamon (0.5g)
- 1/4 cup chopped nuts, such as almonds or walnuts (30g)
- Ground cinnamon for garnish (optional)

Instructions:

1. In a medium saucepan, combine Arborio rice, almond milk, powdered erythritol, vanilla extract, and ground cinnamon.
2. Bring the mixture to a gentle boil over medium heat.
3. Reduce the heat to low and simmer, stirring occasionally, for about 2530 minutes or until the rice is cooked and the pudding thickens.
4. Remove the saucepan from the heat and let the rice pudding cool slightly.
5. Divide the rice pudding into serving bowls.
6. Sprinkle chopped nuts over each bowl.
7. Garnish with a sprinkle of ground cinnamon if desired.
8. Serve warm or chilled and enjoy this comforting sugarfree rice pudding!

Nutritional Info (per serving): Calories: 150 | Fat: 6g | Carbs: 20g | Protein: 4g

KETO CUSTARD TARTS

Prep: 20 mins | Cook: 25 mins | Serves: 6

Ingredients:

- 1 cup almond flour (120g)
- 2 tablespoons powdered erythritol (30g)
- 3 tablespoons unsalted butter, melted (42g)
- 2 large eggs
- 1/2 cup heavy cream (120ml)
- 1/4 cup powdered erythritol (50g)
- 1 teaspoon vanilla extract (5ml)
- Ground nutmeg for garnish (optional)

Instructions:

1. Preheat your oven to 350°F (175°C). Grease a muffin tin or line with paper liners.
2. In a bowl, combine almond flour, 2 tablespoons powdered erythritol, and melted butter. Mix until crumbly.
3. Press the almond flour mixture firmly into the bottom of each muffin cup to form the tart crust.
4. In another bowl, whisk together eggs, heavy cream, 1/4 cup powdered erythritol, and vanilla extract until smooth.
5. Pour the custard mixture evenly into the prepared tart crusts.
6. Sprinkle ground nutmeg over the top of each tart for extra flavor.
7. Bake for 2025 minutes, or until the custard is set and the crust is golden brown.
8. Allow the custard tarts to cool in the muffin tin before serving.
9. Serve at room temperature and enjoy these delightful keto custard tarts!

Nutritional Info (per serving): Calories: 220 | Fat: 20g | Carbs: 6g | Protein: 6g

Prep: 5 mins | Cook: 30 mins | Serves: 4

Ingredients:

- 1/2 cup Arborio rice (100g)
- 2 cups unsweetened almond milk (480ml)
- 2 tablespoons powdered erythritol (30g)
- 1 teaspoon vanilla extract (5ml)
- 1/4 teaspoon ground cinnamon (0.5g)
- 1/4 cup chopped nuts, such as almonds or walnuts (30g)
- Ground cinnamon for garnish (optional)

Instructions:

1. In a medium saucepan, combine Arborio rice, almond milk, powdered erythritol, vanilla extract, and ground cinnamon.
2. Bring the mixture to a gentle boil over medium heat.
3. Reduce the heat to low and simmer, stirring occasionally, for about 2530 minutes or until the rice is cooked and the pudding thickens.
4. Remove the saucepan from the heat and let the rice pudding cool slightly.
5. Divide the rice pudding into serving bowls.
6. Sprinkle chopped nuts over each bowl.
7. Garnish with a sprinkle of ground cinnamon if desired.
8. Serve warm or chilled and enjoy this comforting sugarfree rice pudding!

Nutritional Info (per serving): Calories: 150 | Fat: 6g | Carbs: 20g | Protein: 4g

Prep: 20 mins | Cook: 25 mins | Serves: 6

Ingredients:

- 1 cup almond flour (120g)
- 2 tablespoons powdered erythritol (30g)
- 3 tablespoons unsalted butter, melted (42g)
- 2 large eggs
- 1/2 cup heavy cream (120ml)
- 1/4 cup powdered erythritol (50g)
- 1 teaspoon vanilla extract (5ml)
- Ground nutmeg for garnish (optional)

Instructions:

1. Preheat your oven to 350°F (175°C). Grease a muffin tin or line with paper liners.
2. In a bowl, combine almond flour, 2 tablespoons powdered erythritol, and melted butter. Mix until crumbly.
3. Press the almond flour mixture firmly into the bottom of each muffin cup to form the tart crust.
4. In another bowl, whisk together eggs, heavy cream, 1/4 cup powdered erythritol, and vanilla extract until smooth.
5. Pour the custard mixture evenly into the prepared tart crusts.
6. Sprinkle ground nutmeg over the top of each tart for extra flavor.
7. Bake for 2025 minutes, or until the custard is set and the crust is golden brown.
8. Allow the custard tarts to cool in the muffin tin before serving.
9. Serve at room temperature and enjoy these delightful keto custard tarts!

Nutritional Info (per serving): Calories: 220 | Fat: 20g | Carbs: 6g | Protein: 6g

Prep: 20 mins | Chill: 4 hours | Serves: 6

Ingredients:

- 1 cup brewed espresso, cooled (240ml)
- 2 tablespoons powdered erythritol (30g)
- 1 teaspoon vanilla extract (5ml)
- 8 oz mascarpone cheese, softened (225g)
- 1 cup heavy cream (240ml)
- 2 tablespoons unsweetened cocoa powder (10g)
- Sugar free ladyfinger cookies (approx. 12)
- Unsweetened cocoa powder for dusting

Instructions:

1. In a shallow dish, mix brewed espresso, powdered erythritol, and vanilla extract.
2. In a separate bowl, beat mascarpone cheese until smooth.
3. In another bowl, whip heavy cream until stiff peaks form.
4. Gently fold the whipped cream into the mascarpone cheese until well combined.
5. Dip ladyfinger cookies into the espresso mixture briefly, then arrange them in a single layer in the bottom of a serving dish.
6. Spread half of the mascarpone mixture over the ladyfingers.
7. Repeat the layers with remaining ladyfingers and mascarpone mixture.
8. Dust the top with unsweetened cocoa powder.
9. Cover and refrigerate the tiramisu for at least 4 hours, or overnight, to set.
10. Before serving, dust with additional cocoa powder if desired.
11. Serve chilled and enjoy this decadent lowcarb tiramisu!

Nutritional Info (per serving): Calories: 320 | Fat: 28g | Carbs: 6g | Protein: 7g

CHIA SEED PUDDING

Prep: 5 mins | Chill: 4 hours | Serves: 4

Ingredients:

- 1 cup unsweetened almond milk (240ml)
- 1/4 cup chia seeds (40g)
- 2 tablespoons powdered erythritol (30g)
- 1/2 teaspoon vanilla extract (2.5ml)
- Fresh berries or sliced fruit for topping (optional)

Instructions:

1. In a mixing bowl, whisk together almond milk, chia seeds, powdered erythritol, and vanilla extract until well combined.
2. Cover the bowl and refrigerate for at least 4 hours, or overnight, to allow the chia seeds to thicken.
3. Stir the chia pudding mixture well before serving to distribute the chia seeds evenly.
4. Divide the pudding into serving bowls.
5. Top with fresh berries or sliced fruit if desired.
6. Serve chilled and enjoy this nutritious and satisfying chia seed pudding!

Nutritional Info (per serving): Calories: 90 | Fat: 5g | Carbs: 7g | Protein: 3g

Prep: 20 mins | Cook: 30 mins | Serves: 6

Ingredients:

- 1/2 cup water (120ml)
- 1/4 cup unsalted butter (56g)
- 1/4 teaspoon salt (1.25g)
- 1/2 cup almond flour (60g)
- 2 large eggs
- 1/2 cup heavy cream (120ml)
- 2 tablespoons powdered erythritol (30g)
- 1/2 teaspoon vanilla extract (2.5ml)
- Sugarfree chocolate sauce for drizzling (optional)

Instructions:

1. Preheat your oven to 375°F (190°C). Line a baking sheet with parchment paper.
2. In a saucepan, bring water, butter, and salt to a boil over medium heat.
3. Reduce the heat to low and add almond flour all at once. Stir vigorously until the mixture forms a smooth dough.
4. Remove the saucepan from the heat and let the dough cool slightly.
5. Beat in the eggs, one at a time, mixing well after each addition until the dough is smooth and glossy.
6. Spoon the dough into a piping bag fitted with a large round tip.
7. Pipe the dough into small mounds onto the prepared baking sheet, leaving space between each puff.
8. Bake for 2530 minutes or until the cream puffs are puffed and golden brown.
9. Remove from the oven and let them cool completely on a wire rack.
10. In a separate bowl, whip heavy cream, powdered erythritol, and vanilla extract until stiff peaks form.
11. Slice the cooled cream puffs in half horizontally. Fill each puff with whipped cream.
12. Drizzle with sugarfree chocolate sauce if desired.
13. Serve immediately and enjoy these delightful keto cream puffs!

Nutritional Info (per serving): Calories: 230 | Fat: 21g | Carbs: 3g | Protein: 5g

Prep: 15 mins | Bake: 50 mins | Chill: 4 hours | Serves: 8

Ingredients:

- 1 9inch prebaked lowcarb pie crust
- 1 can (15 oz) pumpkin puree (425g)
- 3/4 cup heavy cream (180ml)
- 2 large eggs
- 1/2 cup powdered erythritol (100g)
- 1 teaspoon ground cinnamon (2g)
- 1/2 teaspoon ground ginger (1g)
- 1/4 teaspoon ground nutmeg (0.5g)
- 1/4 teaspoon salt (1.25g)
- Whipped cream for serving (optional)

Instructions:

1. Preheat your oven to 350°F (175°C).
2. In a large bowl, whisk together pumpkin puree, heavy cream, eggs, powdered erythritol, ground cinnamon, ground ginger, ground nutmeg, and salt until smooth.
3. Pour the pumpkin mixture into the prebaked pie crust.
4. Bake for 4550 minutes or until the center is set.
5. Remove from the oven and let the pie cool completely on a wire rack.
6. Refrigerate for at least 4 hours or overnight to allow the pie to set.
7. Slice and serve with whipped cream if desired.
8. Enjoy this delicious sugarfree pumpkin pie!

Nutritional Info (per serving): Calories: 220 | Fat: 20g | Carbs: 4g | Protein: 4g

Prep: 30 mins | Cook: 15 mins | Chill: 1 hour | Serves: 6

Ingredients:

- 1 cup almond flour (120g)
- 2 tablespoons powdered erythritol (30g)
- 2 tablespoons unsalted butter, melted (28g)
- 1 large egg
- 1/4 teaspoon ground cinnamon (0.5g)
- 1/2 cup ricotta cheese (120g)
- 1/4 cup powdered erythritol (50g)
- 1/2 teaspoon vanilla extract (2.5ml)
- 2 tablespoons chopped dark chocolate or sugarfree chocolate chips (30g)
- Chopped pistachios for garnish (optional)

Instructions:

1. In a mixing bowl, combine almond flour, 2 tablespoons powdered erythritol, melted butter, egg, and ground cinnamon. Mix until a dough forms.
2. Wrap the dough in plastic wrap and refrigerate for 15 minutes.
3. Preheat your oven to 350°F (175°C). Line a baking sheet with parchment paper.
4. Divide the dough into 6 equal portions. Roll each portion into a thin circle between two sheets of parchment paper.
5. Carefully wrap each circle of dough around a cannoli mold or a cylindrical object, overlapping slightly, to form the cannoli shells.
6. Place the wrapped cannoli molds on the prepared baking sheet.
7. Bake for 1215 minutes or until the shells are golden brown.
8. Remove from the oven and let them cool completely on the baking sheet before carefully removing the molds.
9. In a bowl, mix ricotta cheese, 1/4 cup powdered erythritol, and vanilla extract until smooth.
10. Stir in chopped dark chocolate or sugarfree chocolate chips.
11. Fill each cannoli shell with the ricotta mixture using a spoon or piping bag.
12. Garnish the ends with chopped pistachios if desired.
13. Refrigerate the filled cannoli for at least 1 hour to allow the filling to set.
14. Serve chilled and enjoy these delectable keto cannoli!

Nutritional Info (per serving): Calories: 250 | Fat: 20g | Carbs: 6g | Protein: 8g

Prep: 15 mins | Cook: 40 mins | Chill: 4 hours | Serves: 4

Ingredients:

- 1 cup heavy cream (240ml)
- 4 large egg yolks
- 1/4 cup powdered erythritol (50g)
- 1 teaspoon vanilla extract (5ml)
- 2 tablespoons powdered erythritol, for caramelizing (30g)

Instructions:

1. Preheat your oven to 325°F (160°C).
2. In a saucepan, heat heavy cream over medium heat until it just begins to simmer. Remove from heat and let it cool slightly.
3. In a mixing bowl, whisk together egg yolks, 1/4 cup powdered erythritol, and vanilla extract until smooth and creamy.
4. Slowly pour the warm heavy cream into the egg mixture, whisking continuously to prevent curdling.
5. Strain the custard mixture through a finemesh sieve into a measuring cup or bowl.
6. Divide the custard among four ramekins or custard cups.
7. Place the ramekins in a baking dish and fill the dish with enough hot water to reach halfway up the sides of the ramekins.
8. Bake for 3540 minutes or until the custard is set but still slightly jiggly in the center.
9. Remove the ramekins from the water bath and let them cool to room temperature.
10. Refrigerate for at least 4 hours or overnight to chill and set completely.
11. Just before serving, sprinkle about 1/2 tablespoon of powdered erythritol evenly over the surface of each custard.
12. Caramelize the erythritol using a kitchen torch until golden and bubbly.
13. Let the caramelized sugar harden for a minute before serving.
14. Serve and enjoy this elegant lowcarb crème brûlée!

Nutritional Info (per serving): Calories: 330 | Fat: 30g | Carbs: 3g | Protein: 5g

Prep: 15 mins | Chill: 2 hours | Serves: 4

Ingredients:

- 1 cup heavy cream (240ml)
- 2 tablespoons powdered erythritol (30g)
- 2 tablespoons unsweetened cocoa powder (10g)
- 1/2 teaspoon vanilla extract (2.5ml)
- Sugarfree chocolate shavings for garnish (optional)

Instructions:

1. In a mixing bowl, whip heavy cream until soft peaks form.
2. Add powdered erythritol, unsweetened cocoa powder, and vanilla extract to the whipped cream.
3. Continue whipping until stiff peaks form and the mixture is smooth and fluffy.
4. Spoon the chocolate mousse into serving cups or glasses.
5. Refrigerate for at least 2 hours to allow the mousse to set.
6. Before serving, garnish with sugarfree chocolate shavings if desired.
7. Serve chilled and enjoy these decadent keto chocolate mousse cups!

Nutritional Info (per serving): Calories: 220 | Fat: 23g | Carbs: 3g | Protein: 2g

Prep: 15 mins | Cook: 50 mins | Chill: 4 hours | Serves: 6

Ingredients:

- 1/2 cup powdered erythritol (100g)
- 1/4 cup water (60ml)
- 1 can (14 oz) unsweetened coconut milk (400ml)
- 3 large eggs
- 1 teaspoon vanilla extract (5ml)

Instructions:

1. Preheat your oven to 325°F (160°C).
2. In a small saucepan, combine powdered erythritol and water. Heat over medium heat until the erythritol is dissolved, stirring occasionally.
3. Pour the erythritol syrup into the bottom of a round baking dish, swirling to coat the bottom evenly.
4. In a mixing bowl, whisk together coconut milk, eggs, and vanilla extract until well combined.
5. Pour the coconut milk mixture over the erythritol syrup in the baking dish.
6. Place the baking dish in a larger baking pan. Fill the larger pan with hot water until it reaches halfway up the sides of the flan dish.
7. Bake for 4550 minutes or until the flan is set but still slightly jiggly in the center.
8. Remove the flan from the water bath and let it cool to room temperature.
9. Refrigerate for at least 4 hours or overnight to chill and set completely.
10. To serve, run a knife around the edge of the flan to loosen it. Invert onto a serving plate.
11. Slice and serve chilled slices of this delightful sugarfree flan!

Nutritional Info (per serving): Calories: 160 | Fat: 15g | Carbs: 2g | Protein: 4g

Prep: 20 mins | Cook: 40 mins | Chill: 4 hours | Serves: 9

Ingredients:

- 1 1/2 cups almond flour (180g)
- 1/4 cup powdered erythritol (50g)
- 1/4 cup unsalted butter, melted (56g)
- 16 oz cream cheese, softened (450g)
- 1/2 cup powdered erythritol (100g)
- 2 large eggs
- 1 teaspoon vanilla extract (5ml)
- Sugar free fruit preserves for topping (optional)

Instructions:

1. Preheat your oven to 325°F (160°C). Line an 8x8inch baking pan with parchment paper, leaving an overhang on the sides.
2. In a bowl, combine almond flour, 1/4 cup powdered erythritol, and melted butter. Mix until crumbly.
3. Press the almond flour mixture firmly into the bottom of the prepared baking pan to form the crust.
4. Bake the crust for 1012 minutes or until lightly golden. Remove from the oven and let it cool slightly.
5. In a mixing bowl, beat cream cheese, 1/2 cup powdered erythritol, eggs, and vanilla extract until smooth and creamy.
6. Pour the cream cheese mixture over the baked crust, spreading it evenly.
7. Return the pan to the oven and bake for 2530 minutes or until the cheesecake is set.
8. Remove from the oven and let it cool to room temperature.
9. Refrigerate for at least 4 hours or until chilled and firm.
10. Once chilled, lift the cheesecake bars out of the pan using the parchment paper overhang.
11. Slice into bars and top each with a dollop of sugarfree fruit preserves if desired.
12. Serve chilled and enjoy these scrumptious lowcarb cheesecake bars!

Nutritional Info (per serving): Calories: 260 | Fat: 24g | Carbs: 4g | Protein: 6g

KETO CHOCOLATE CAKE

Prep: 15 mins | Bake: 30 mins | Serves: 12

Ingredients:

- 1 1/2 cups almond flour (180g)
- 1/2 cup unsweetened cocoa powder (50g)
- 1/4 cup powdered erythritol (50g)
- 1 teaspoon baking powder (5g)
- 1/2 teaspoon baking soda (2.5g)
- 1/4 teaspoon salt (1.25g)
- 4 large eggs
- 1/2 cup unsweetened almond milk (120ml)
- 1/4 cup melted coconut oil (56g)
- 1 teaspoon vanilla extract (5ml)
- Sugar free chocolate chips for garnish (optional)

Instructions:

1. Preheat your oven to 350°F (175°C). Grease and line a round cake pan with parchment paper.
2. In a large bowl, whisk together almond flour, cocoa powder, powdered erythritol, baking powder, baking soda, and salt.
3. In a separate bowl, beat eggs, almond milk, melted coconut oil, and vanilla extract until well combined.
4. Gradually add the wet ingredients to the dry ingredients, mixing until smooth and no lumps remain.
5. Pour the batter into the prepared cake pan, spreading it evenly.
6. Bake for 2530 minutes or until a toothpick inserted into the center comes out clean.
7. Remove from the oven and let the cake cool in the pan for 10 minutes before transferring it to a wire rack to cool completely.
8. Once cooled, garnish with sugarfree chocolate chips if desired.
9. Slice and serve this decadent keto chocolate cake!

Nutritional Info (per serving): Calories: 180 | Fat: 15g | Carbs: 5g | Protein: 7g

LOWCARB CHOCOLATE CHIP COOKIES

Prep: 10 mins | Bake: 12 mins | Serves: 24 cookies

Ingredients:

- 1 1/2 cups almond flour (180g)
- 1/4 cup coconut flour (30g)
- 1/4 cup powdered erythritol (50g)
- 1/2 teaspoon baking soda (2.5g)
- 1/4 teaspoon salt (1.25g)
- 1/3 cup melted coconut oil (75g)
- 1 large egg
- 1 teaspoon vanilla extract (5ml)
- 1/2 cup sugar free chocolate chips (90g)

Instructions:

1. Preheat your oven to 350°F (175°C). Line a baking sheet with parchment paper.
2. In a large bowl, combine almond flour, coconut flour, powdered erythritol, baking soda, and salt.
3. In a separate bowl, whisk together melted coconut oil, egg, and vanilla extract.
4. Gradually add the wet ingredients to the dry ingredients, mixing until a dough forms.
5. Fold in sugarfree chocolate chips until evenly distributed.
6. Scoop the dough onto the prepared baking sheet, spacing the cookies evenly apart.
7. Gently flatten each cookie with the back of a spoon or your fingertips.
8. Bake for 1012 minutes or until the edges are golden brown.
9. Remove from the oven and let the cookies cool on the baking sheet for 5 minutes before transferring them to a wire rack to cool completely.
10. Enjoy these delightful lowcarb chocolate chip cookies with a glass of unsweetened almond milk!

Nutritional Info (per cookie): Calories: 90 | Fat: 8g | Carbs: 3g | Protein: 2g

SUGARFREE CHOCOLATE TRUFFLES

Prep: 15 mins | Chill: 2 hours | Serves: 12 truffles

Ingredients:

- 1/2 cup heavy cream (120ml)
- 1 cup sugarfree dark chocolate chips (180g)
- 1 teaspoon vanilla extract (5ml)
- Unsweetened cocoa powder or shredded coconut, for coating (optional)

Instructions:

1. In a small saucepan, heat heavy cream over medium heat until it just begins to simmer.
2. Place sugarfree dark chocolate chips in a heatproof bowl.
3. Pour the hot cream over the chocolate chips and let it sit for 1 minute.
4. Stir the mixture until the chocolate is completely melted and smooth.
5. Stir in vanilla extract until well combined.
6. Cover the bowl and refrigerate the chocolate mixture for at least 2 hours or until firm.
7. Once chilled, use a spoon or small scoop to portion out the chocolate mixture and roll it into balls.
8. Roll the truffles in unsweetened cocoa powder or shredded coconut for coating, if desired.
9. Place the coated truffles on a parchmentlined baking sheet.
10. Chill the truffles in the refrigerator for an additional 30 minutes to set.
11. Serve these indulgent sugarfree chocolate truffles chilled and enjoy!

Nutritional Info (per truffle): Calories: 70 | Fat: 6g | Carbs: 2g | Protein: 1g

Prep: 15 mins | Chill: 2 hours | Serves: 4

Ingredients:

- 1 cup heavy cream (240ml)
- 1/4 cup powdered erythritol (50g)
- 1/4 cup unsweetened cocoa powder (25g)
- 1 teaspoon vanilla extract (5ml)
- Sugarfree whipped cream, for topping (optional)
- Sugarfree chocolate shavings, for garnish (optional)

Instructions:

1. In a mixing bowl, whip heavy cream until soft peaks form.
2. Add powdered erythritol, unsweetened cocoa powder, and vanilla extract to the whipped cream.
3. Continue whipping until stiff peaks form and the mixture is smooth and fluffy.
4. Divide the chocolate mousse into serving cups or glasses.
5. Refrigerate for at least 2 hours to allow the mousse to set.
6. Before serving, top with sugarfree whipped cream and garnish with sugarfree chocolate shavings, if desired.
7. Serve chilled and indulge in this decadent keto chocolate mousse!

Nutritional Info (per serving): Calories: 220 | Fat: 20g | Carbs: 3g | Protein: 2g

Prep: 5 mins | Cook: 5 mins | Serves: 2

Ingredients:

- 2 cups unsweetened almond milk (480ml)
- 2 tablespoons unsweetened cocoa powder (10g)
- 2 tablespoons powdered erythritol (30g)
- 1/2 teaspoon vanilla extract (2.5ml)
- Sugarfree whipped cream, for topping (optional)
- Sugarfree chocolate shavings, for garnish (optional)

Instructions:

1. In a small saucepan, heat unsweetened almond milk over medium heat until warmed through.
2. Whisk in unsweetened cocoa powder and powdered erythritol until fully dissolved and smooth.
3. Stir in vanilla extract and continue to heat until the hot chocolate reaches your desired temperature.
4. Remove from heat and pour the hot chocolate into mugs.
5. Top with sugarfree whipped cream and garnish with sugarfree chocolate shavings, if desired.
6. Serve immediately and enjoy this comforting sugarfree hot chocolate!

Nutritional Info (per serving): Calories: 40 | Fat: 3g | Carbs: 2g | Protein: 1g

LOWCARB CHOCOLATE BROWNIES

Prep: 10 mins | Bake: 25 mins | Serves: 9

Ingredients:

- 1/2 cup almond flour (60g)
- 1/4 cup unsweetened cocoa powder (25g)
- 1/2 teaspoon baking powder (2.5g)
- 1/4 teaspoon salt (1.25g)
- 1/3 cup powdered erythritol (65g)
- 1/4 cup melted coconut oil (56g)
- 2 large eggs
- 1 teaspoon vanilla extract (5ml)
- Sugar free chocolate chips for topping (optional)

Instructions:

1. Preheat your oven to 350°F (175°C). Grease and line an 8x8inch baking pan with parchment paper.
2. In a mixing bowl, combine almond flour, unsweetened cocoa powder, baking powder, salt, and powdered erythritol.
3. In a separate bowl, whisk together melted coconut oil, eggs, and vanilla extract.
4. Gradually add the wet ingredients to the dry ingredients, mixing until smooth.
5. Pour the batter into the prepared baking pan, spreading it evenly.
6. Sprinkle sugarfree chocolate chips over the top, if desired.
7. Bake for 2025 minutes or until a toothpick inserted into the center comes out with moist crumbs.
8. Remove from the oven and let the brownies cool in the pan before slicing into squares.
9. Serve these indulgent lowcarb chocolate brownies and enjoy!

Nutritional Info (per serving): Calories: 120 | Fat: 10g | Carbs: 4g | Protein: 3g

Prep: 15 mins | Bake: 20 mins | Serves: 12 cupcakes

Ingredients:

- 1 1/2 cups almond flour (180g)
- 1/4 cup unsweetened cocoa powder (25g)
- 1/4 cup powdered erythritol (50g)
- 1 teaspoon baking powder (5g)
- 1/4 teaspoon salt (1.25g)
- 1/3 cup melted coconut oil (75g)
- 3 large eggs
- 1/2 cup unsweetened almond milk (120ml)
- 1 teaspoon vanilla extract (5ml)

Instructions:

1. Preheat your oven to 350°F (175°C). Line a muffin tin with paper liners.
2. In a mixing bowl, whisk together almond flour, unsweetened cocoa powder, powdered erythritol, baking powder, and salt.
3. In a separate bowl, whisk together melted coconut oil, eggs, almond milk, and vanilla extract.
4. Gradually add the wet ingredients to the dry ingredients, mixing until smooth.
5. Spoon the batter into the prepared muffin tin, filling each liner about twothirds full.
6. Bake for 1820 minutes or until a toothpick inserted into the center comes out clean.
7. Remove from the oven and let the cupcakes cool in the pan for 5 minutes before transferring them to a wire rack to cool completely.
8. Once cooled, frost with sugarfree frosting or ganache, if desired.
9. Enjoy these delightful keto chocolate cupcakes as a guiltfree treat!

Nutritional Info (per cupcake): Calories: 120 | Fat: 10g | Carbs: 3g | Protein: 4g

Prep: 10 mins | Cook: 10 mins | Chill: 2 hours | Serves: 4

Ingredients:

- 2 cups unsweetened almond milk (480ml)
- 1/4 cup unsweetened cocoa powder (25g)
- 1/4 cup powdered erythritol (50g)
- 2 tablespoons cornstarch (16g)
- 1/4 teaspoon salt (1.25g)
- 1 teaspoon vanilla extract (5ml)
- Sugar free whipped cream, for topping (optional)

Instructions:

1. In a saucepan, whisk together unsweetened almond milk, cocoa powder, powdered erythritol, cornstarch, and salt until smooth.
2. Place the saucepan over medium heat and cook, stirring constantly, until the mixture thickens and comes to a gentle boil.
3. Reduce the heat to low and continue to cook for an additional 2 minutes, stirring continuously.
4. Remove from heat and stir in vanilla extract until well combined.
5. Divide the chocolate pudding among serving cups or bowls.
6. Cover each cup with plastic wrap, pressing it directly onto the surface of the pudding to prevent a skin from forming.
7. Refrigerate for at least 2 hours or until the pudding is chilled and set.
8. Before serving, top with sugarfree whipped cream if desired.
9. Enjoy this creamy and delicious sugarfree chocolate pudding!

Nutritional Info (per serving): Calories: 50 | Fat: 3g | Carbs: 4g | Protein: 2g

Prep: 20 mins | Chill: 2 hours | Serves: 8

Ingredients:

- 1 1/2 cups almond flour (180g)
- 1/4 cup unsweetened cocoa powder (25g)
- 1/4 cup powdered erythritol (50g)
- 1/4 teaspoon salt (1.25g)
- 1/3 cup melted coconut oil (75g)
- 1 teaspoon vanilla extract (5ml)
- 1/2 cup sugar free chocolate chips (90g)
- 1/4 cup heavy cream (60ml)
- Sugarfree whipped cream, for topping (optional)
- Fresh berries, for garnish (optional)

Instructions:

1. In a mixing bowl, combine almond flour, unsweetened cocoa powder, powdered erythritol, and salt.
2. Stir in melted coconut oil and vanilla extract until a dough forms.
3. Press the dough evenly into the bottom and up the sides of a tart pan.
4. Place the tart pan in the freezer while you prepare the chocolate filling.
5. In a heatproof bowl, combine sugarfree chocolate chips and heavy cream.
6. Microwave in 30second intervals, stirring between each, until the chocolate is melted and smooth.
7. Pour the chocolate filling into the chilled tart crust.
8. Smooth the top with a spatula and refrigerate for at least 2 hours or until set.
9. Once set, remove the tart from the pan and garnish with sugarfree whipped cream and fresh berries, if desired.
10. Slice and serve this elegant lowcarb chocolate tart!

Nutritional Info (per serving): Calories: 220 | Fat: 20g | Carbs: 6g | Protein: 4g

KETO CHOCOLATE LAVA CAKES

Prep: 15 mins | Bake: 12 mins | Serves: 4

Ingredients:

- 1/2 cup sugarfree dark chocolate chips (90g)
- 1/4 cup unsalted butter (56g)
- 2 large eggs
- 2 tablespoons powdered erythritol (30g)
- 1 teaspoon vanilla extract (5ml)
- 2 tablespoons almond flour (15g)
- Pinch of salt (optional)
- Sugar free whipped cream, for serving (optional)
- Fresh berries, for garnish (optional)

Instructions:

1. Preheat your oven to 425°F (220°C). Grease four ramekins and place them on a baking sheet.
2. In a microwavesafe bowl, combine sugarfree dark chocolate chips and unsalted butter.
3. Microwave in 30second intervals, stirring between each, until melted and smooth.
4. In a separate bowl, whisk together eggs, powdered erythritol, and vanilla extract until well combined.
5. Gradually whisk the melted chocolate mixture into the egg mixture until smooth.
6. Stir in almond flour and a pinch of salt until fully incorporated.
7. Divide the batter evenly among the prepared ramekins.
8. Bake for 1012 minutes or until the edges are set but the centers are still soft.
9. Remove from the oven and let the lava cakes cool in the ramekins for 2 minutes.
10. Carefully invert each lava cake onto a serving plate.
11. Serve immediately with sugarfree whipped cream and fresh berries, if desired.
12. Enjoy these indulgent keto chocolate lava cakes while warm!

Nutritional Info (per serving): Calories: 220 | Fat: 18g | Carbs: 7g | Protein: 6g

SUGARFREE CHOCOLATE MILKSHAKE

Prep: 5 mins | Serves: 2

Ingredients:

- 2 cups unsweetened almond milk (480ml)
- 1/4 cup unsweetened cocoa powder (25g)
- 2 tablespoons powdered erythritol (30g)
- 1 teaspoon vanilla extract (5ml)
- 2 cups ice cubes
- Sugarfree whipped cream, for topping (optional)
- Sugarfree chocolate shavings, for garnish (optional)

Instructions:

1. In a blender, combine unsweetened almond milk, unsweetened cocoa powder, powdered erythritol, and vanilla extract.
2. Add ice cubes to the blender.
3. Blend until smooth and creamy.
4. Pour the chocolate milkshake into glasses.
5. Top with sugarfree whipped cream and garnish with sugarfree chocolate shavings, if desired.
6. Serve immediately and enjoy this delicious and refreshing sugarfree chocolate milkshake!

Nutritional Info (per serving): Calories: 40 | Fat: 3g | Carbs: 2g | Protein: 1g

Prep: 20 mins | Chill: 4 hours | Serves: 8

Ingredients:

- 1 1/2 cups almond flour (180g)
- 1/4 cup unsweetened cocoa powder (25g)
- 1/4 cup powdered erythritol (50g)
- 1/4 teaspoon salt (1.25g)
- 1/3 cup melted coconut oil (75g)
- 1 teaspoon vanilla extract (5ml)
- 1 cup heavy cream (240ml)
- 4 ounces sugar free dark chocolate, chopped (115g)
- Sugar free whipped cream, for topping (optional)
- Sugar free chocolate shavings, for garnish (optional)

Instructions:

1. In a mixing bowl, combine almond flour, unsweetened cocoa powder, powdered erythritol, and salt.
2. Stir in melted coconut oil and vanilla extract until a dough forms.
3. Press the dough evenly into the bottom and up the sides of a pie dish.
4. Bake the crust at 350°F (175°C) for 1012 minutes or until set. Let it cool completely.
5. In a saucepan, heat heavy cream over medium heat until it just begins to simmer.
6. Remove from heat and add chopped sugarfree dark chocolate to the hot cream.
7. Let it sit for 2 minutes, then stir until the chocolate is completely melted and the mixture is smooth.
8. Pour the chocolate filling into the cooled pie crust.
9. Refrigerate for at least 4 hours or until the filling is set.
10. Once set, top with sugarfree whipped cream and garnish with sugarfree chocolate shavings, if desired.
11. Slice and serve this luscious lowcarb chocolate cream pie!

Nutritional Info (per serving): Calories: 270 | Fat: 24g | Carbs: 6g | Protein: 4g

KETO CHOCOLATE BISCOTTI

Prep: 15 mins | Bake: 25 mins | Serves: 12 biscotti

Ingredients:

- 1 1/2 cups almond flour (180g)
- 1/4 cup unsweetened cocoa powder (25g)
- 1/4 cup powdered erythritol (50g)
- 1 teaspoon baking powder (5g)
- 1/4 teaspoon salt (1.25g)
- 2 tablespoons melted coconut oil (28g)
- 1 large egg
- 1 teaspoon vanilla extract (5ml)
- 1/4 cup sugarfree chocolate chips (45g)

Instructions:

1. Preheat your oven to 350°F (175°C). Line a baking sheet with parchment paper.
2. In a mixing bowl, combine almond flour, unsweetened cocoa powder, powdered erythritol, baking powder, and salt.
3. In a separate bowl, whisk together melted coconut oil, egg, and vanilla extract.
4. Gradually add the wet ingredients to the dry ingredients, mixing until a dough forms.
5. Fold in sugarfree chocolate chips until evenly distributed.
6. Transfer the dough to the prepared baking sheet and shape it into a log about 12 inches long and 4 inches wide.
7. Bake for 2025 minutes or until the log is firm to the touch.
8. Remove from the oven and let it cool on the baking sheet for 10 minutes.
9. Reduce the oven temperature to 325°F (160°C).
10. Transfer the cooled log to a cutting board and slice it diagonally into 12 biscotti.
11. Place the biscotti cutside down on the baking sheet and bake for an additional 10 minutes.
12. Remove from the oven and let the biscotti cool completely on a wire rack.
13. Serve these crunchy keto chocolate biscotti with a cup of coffee or tea!

Nutritional Info (per biscotti): Calories: 110 | Fat: 9g | Carbs: 4g | Protein: 3g

SUGARFREE CHOCOLATE FONDUE

Prep: 5 mins | Cook: 5 mins | Serves: 4

Ingredients:
- 1/2 cup heavy cream (120ml)
- 1 cup sugarfree dark chocolate chips (180g)
- 1/2 teaspoon vanilla extract (2.5ml)
- Assorted lowcarb dippers, such as strawberries, raspberries, sliced apples, or cubes of lowcarb pound cake

Instructions:
1. In a small saucepan, heat heavy cream over medium heat until it just begins to simmer.
2. Reduce the heat to low and stir in sugarfree dark chocolate chips until melted and smooth.
3. Stir in vanilla extract until well combined.
4. Transfer the chocolate fondue to a serving bowl or fondue pot.
5. Arrange assorted lowcarb dippers on a platter.
6. Serve the chocolate fondue with the dippers and enjoy dipping!

Nutritional Info (per serving without dippers): Calories: 220 | Fat: 20g | Carbs: 6g | Protein: 2g

LOWCARB CHOCOLATE HAZELNUT COOKIES

Prep: 15 mins | Bake: 12 mins | Serves: 24 cookies

Ingredients:

- 1 1/2 cups almond flour (180g)
- 1/4 cup unsweetened cocoa powder (25g)
- 1/4 cup powdered erythritol (50g)
- 1/2 teaspoon baking powder (2.5g)
- 1/4 teaspoon salt (1.25g)
- 1/3 cup melted coconut oil (75g)
- 1 large egg
- 1 teaspoon vanilla extract (5ml)
- 1/4 cup sugarfree chocolate chips (45g)
- 1/4 cup chopped hazelnuts (30g)

Instructions:

1. Preheat your oven to 350°F (175°C). Line a baking sheet with parchment paper.
2. In a mixing bowl, combine almond flour, unsweetened cocoa powder, powdered erythritol, baking powder, and salt.
3. In a separate bowl, whisk together melted coconut oil, egg, and vanilla extract.
4. Gradually add the wet ingredients to the dry ingredients, mixing until a dough forms.
5. Fold in sugarfree chocolate chips and chopped hazelnuts until evenly distributed.
6. Scoop the dough onto the prepared baking sheet, spacing the cookies evenly apart.
7. Gently flatten each cookie with the back of a spoon or your fingertips.
8. Bake for 1012 minutes or until the edges are set.
9. Remove from the oven and let the cookies cool on the baking sheet for 5 minutes before transferring them to a wire rack to cool completely.
10. Enjoy these delightful lowcarb chocolate hazelnut cookies with a glass of unsweetened almond milk!

Nutritional Info (per cookie): Calories: 80 | Fat: 7g | Carbs: 3g | Protein: 2g

ALMOND FLOUR COOKIES

Prep: 15 mins | Cook: 12 mins | Makes: 24 cookies

Ingredients:

- 2 cups almond flour (200g)
- 1/4 cup unsalted butter, softened (57g)
- 1/4 cup powdered erythritol (50g)
- 1 large egg
- 1 teaspoon vanilla extract (5ml)
- 1/4 teaspoon baking soda (1.25g)
- Pinch of salt (optional)

Instructions:

1. Preheat your oven to 350°F (175°C) and line a baking sheet with parchment paper.
2. In a mixing bowl, cream together the softened unsalted butter and powdered erythritol until smooth.
3. Add the egg and vanilla extract, and beat until well combined.
4. Gradually add the almond flour, baking soda, and a pinch of salt (if using), mixing until a dough forms.
5. Roll the dough into 1inch balls and place them on the prepared baking sheet.
6. Flatten each ball with the palm of your hand or the bottom of a glass.
7. Bake in the preheated oven for 1012 minutes or until the edges are golden brown.
8. Remove from the oven and let the cookies cool on the baking sheet for 5 minutes.
9. Transfer the cookies to a wire rack to cool completely before serving.

Nutritional Info (per cookie): Calories: 80 | Fat: 7g | Carbs: 3g | Protein: 2g

PECAN SANDIES

Prep: 10 mins | Cook: 15 mins | Makes: 18 cookies

Ingredients:

- 1 cup almond flour (100g)
- 1/2 cup chopped pecans (60g)
- 1/4 cup unsalted butter, softened (57g)
- 1/4 cup powdered erythritol (50g)
- 1 teaspoon vanilla extract (5ml)
- 1/4 teaspoon baking soda (1.25g)
- Pinch of salt (optional)

Instructions:

1. Preheat your oven to 325°F (160°C) and line a baking sheet with parchment paper.
2. In a mixing bowl, cream together the softened unsalted butter and powdered erythritol until smooth.
3. Add the vanilla extract, and beat until well combined.
4. Gradually add the almond flour, chopped pecans, baking soda, and a pinch of salt (if using), mixing until a dough forms.
5. Roll the dough into balls and place them on the prepared baking sheet.
6. Flatten each ball slightly with the palm of your hand.
7. Bake in the preheated oven for 1215 minutes or until the cookies are lightly golden brown.
8. Remove from the oven and let the cookies cool on the baking sheet for 5 minutes.
9. Transfer the cookies to a wire rack to cool completely before serving.

Nutritional Info (per cookie): Calories: 90 | Fat: 8g | Carbs: 2g | Protein: 2g

KETO PEANUT BUTTER CUPS

Prep: 15 mins | Chill: 30 mins | Makes: 12 servings

Ingredients:

- 1/2 cup sugarfree peanut butter (120g)
- 2 tablespoons powdered erythritol (30g)
- 1/4 cup coconut oil, melted (60ml)
- 1/4 cup unsweetened cocoa powder (25g)
- 2 tablespoons powdered erythritol (30g)
- 1/2 teaspoon vanilla extract (2.5ml)
- Pinch of salt (optional)

Instructions:

1. In a mixing bowl, combine the sugarfree peanut butter and 2 tablespoons of powdered erythritol until smooth.
2. In a separate bowl, mix together the melted coconut oil, unsweetened cocoa powder, remaining 2 tablespoons of powdered erythritol, vanilla extract, and a pinch of salt (if using) until well combined.
3. Line a mini muffin tin with paper liners.
4. Spoon a small amount of the chocolate mixture into each paper liner, covering the bottom.
5. Place the muffin tin in the freezer for 10 minutes to set the chocolate layer.
6. Remove the muffin tin from the freezer and spoon a small amount of the peanut butter mixture on top of the chocolate layer in each paper liner.
7. Place the muffin tin back in the freezer for another 10 minutes to set the peanut butter layer.
8. Finally, spoon the remaining chocolate mixture over the peanut butter layer in each paper liner, covering completely.
9. Return the muffin tin to the freezer for a final 10 minutes to set the top chocolate layer.
10. Once set, remove the peanut butter cups from the muffin tin and store them in an airtight container in the refrigerator.
11. Enjoy these homemade keto peanut butter cups as a guiltfree treat!

Nutritional Info (per serving 1 peanut butter cup): Calories: 120 | Fat: 11g | Carbs: 3g | Protein: 3g

CHIA SEED PUDDING

Prep: 5 mins | Chill: 2 hours | Serves: 2

Ingredients:

- 1 cup unsweetened almond milk (240ml)
- 1/4 cup chia seeds (40g)
- 2 tablespoons powdered erythritol (30g)
- 1/2 teaspoon vanilla extract (2.5ml)
- Sugar free berries, for topping (optional)

Instructions:

1. In a mixing bowl, combine the unsweetened almond milk, chia seeds, powdered erythritol, and vanilla extract.
2. Whisk the ingredients together until well combined.
3. Let the mixture sit for 5 minutes, then whisk again to prevent clumps.
4. Cover the bowl and refrigerate for at least 2 hours or overnight, allowing the chia seeds to thicken and absorb the liquid.
5. Once chilled and thickened, give the pudding a final stir to break up any clumps.
6. Divide the chia seed pudding into serving glasses or bowls.
7. Top with sugarfree berries, if desired, and serve chilled.
8. Enjoy this creamy and nutritious chia seed pudding as a satisfying dessert or breakfast option!

Nutritional Info (per serving): Calories: 90 | Fat: 6g | Carbs: 6g | Protein: 3g

LOWCARB BAKLAVA

Prep: 30 mins | Bake: 25 mins | Serves: 12 pieces

Ingredients:

- 1 cup chopped mixed nuts (such as walnuts, almonds, and pistachios) (120g)
- 1/4 cup powdered erythritol (50g)
- 1 teaspoon ground cinnamon (2.5g)
- 1/4 teaspoon ground cloves (0.6g)
- 1/4 cup melted unsalted butter (57g)
- 8 sheets phyllo dough, thawed if frozen
- Sugarfree syrup, for drizzling (optional)

Instructions:

1. Preheat your oven to 350°F (175°C) and grease a baking dish with melted unsalted butter.
2. In a mixing bowl, combine the chopped mixed nuts, powdered erythritol, ground cinnamon, and ground cloves. Mix well.
3. Lay one sheet of phyllo dough in the prepared baking dish and brush it with melted unsalted butter.
4. Repeat the process, layering and buttering each sheet of phyllo dough until you have used half of the sheets.
5. Spread the nut mixture evenly over the layered phyllo dough.
6. Continue layering the remaining sheets of phyllo dough on top of the nut mixture, brushing each sheet with melted unsalted butter.
7. Using a sharp knife, cut the baklava into squares or diamonds.
8. Bake in the preheated oven for 25 minutes or until golden brown and crispy.
9. Remove from the oven and let it cool in the baking dish for 5 minutes.
10. Drizzle sugarfree syrup over the baklava, if desired, and let it cool completely before serving.

Nutritional Info (per piece): Calories: 150 | Fat: 13g | Carbs: 4g | Protein: 3g

Prep: 15 mins | Bake: 30 mins | Serves: 12 bars

Ingredients:

- 1 1/2 cups almond flour (180g)
- 1/4 cup powdered erythritol (50g)
- 1/4 teaspoon salt (1.25g)
- 1/3 cup unsalted butter, melted (75g)
- 1/2 cup sugarfree maple syrup (120ml)
- 2 large eggs
- 1 teaspoon vanilla extract (5ml)
- 1 1/2 cups chopped pecans (180g)

Instructions:

1. Preheat your oven to 350°F (175°C) and line a baking dish with parchment paper.
2. In a mixing bowl, combine almond flour, powdered erythritol, and salt.
3. Stir in melted unsalted butter until a crumbly dough forms.
4. Press the dough evenly into the bottom of the prepared baking dish.
5. Bake the crust in the preheated oven for 10 minutes.
6. In another mixing bowl, whisk together sugarfree maple syrup, eggs, and vanilla extract until well combined.
7. Stir in chopped pecans.
8. Pour the pecan mixture over the partially baked crust.
9. Return the baking dish to the oven and bake for an additional 20 minutes or until the filling is set.
10. Remove from the oven and let it cool completely in the baking dish.
11. Once cooled, lift the parchment paper to remove the bars from the baking dish and transfer them to a cutting board.
12. Cut into bars and serve.

Nutritional Info (per bar): Calories: 180 | Fat: 16g | Carbs: 5g | Protein: 4g

Prep: 15 mins | Cook: 5 mins | Makes: 1 cup

Ingredients:

- 1 cup roasted hazelnuts (120g)
- 2 tablespoons powdered erythritol (30g)
- 2 tablespoons unsweetened cocoa powder (10g)
- 2 tablespoons melted coconut oil (30ml)
- 1/2 teaspoon vanilla extract (2.5ml)
- Pinch of salt (optional)
- Liquid stevia, to taste (optional)

Instructions:

1. Preheat your oven to 350°F (175°C) and spread the hazelnuts on a baking sheet in a single layer.
2. Roast the hazelnuts in the preheated oven for 1012 minutes or until fragrant and lightly browned.
3. Remove the hazelnuts from the oven and let them cool slightly.
4. Place the roasted hazelnuts in a clean kitchen towel and rub them together to remove the skins.
5. Transfer the peeled hazelnuts to a food processor.
6. Add powdered erythritol, unsweetened cocoa powder, melted coconut oil, vanilla extract, and a pinch of salt (if using) to the food processor.
7. Process the mixture until smooth and creamy, scraping down the sides of the bowl as needed.
8. Taste the hazelnut spread and adjust the sweetness with liquid stevia, if desired.
9. Transfer the sugarfree hazelnut spread to a jar or airtight container and store it in the refrigerator.
10. Enjoy this homemade sugarfree hazelnut spread on toast, pancakes, or as a dip for fruit.

Nutritional Info (per tablespoon): Calories: 100 | Fat: 9g | Carbs: 2g | Protein: 2g

Prep: 10 mins | Chill: 2 hours | Serves: 16 pieces

Ingredients:

- 1 cup unsalted cashew butter (240g)
- 1/4 cup coconut oil, melted (60ml)
- 1/4 cup powdered erythritol (50g)
- 1 teaspoon vanilla extract (5ml)
- Pinch of salt (optional)
- 2 tablespoons unsweetened cocoa powder (10g), for chocolate flavor (optional)

Instructions:

1. Line a small baking dish or container with parchment paper, leaving some overhang on the sides for easy removal.
2. In a mixing bowl, combine unsalted cashew butter, melted coconut oil, powdered erythritol, vanilla extract, and a pinch of salt (if using). Mix until smooth and well combined.
3. If making chocolate fudge, divide the mixture in half. Stir the unsweetened cocoa powder into one half of the mixture until fully incorporated.
4. Pour the cashew butter mixture (or half of it for chocolate fudge) into the prepared baking dish.
5. Use a spatula to spread the mixture evenly in the dish, smoothing the top.
6. Place the baking dish in the refrigerator and chill for at least 2 hours or until the fudge is set.
7. Once set, use the parchment paper overhang to lift the fudge out of the dish.
8. Cut the fudge into squares or rectangles.
9. Serve immediately, or store the fudge in an airtight container in the refrigerator for up to 1 week.

Nutritional Info (per piece): Calories: 120 | Fat: 11g | Carbs: 3g | Protein: 2g

Prep: 10 mins | Cook: 10 mins | Chill: 1 hour | Serves: 8

Ingredients:

- 1 cup unsalted pistachios, shelled (120g)
- 1/4 cup powdered erythritol (50g)
- 2 tablespoons unsalted butter (28g)
- 2 tablespoons water (30ml)
- 1/4 teaspoon vanilla extract (1.25ml)
- Pinch of salt (optional)
- 1/4 teaspoon baking soda (1.25g)

Instructions:

1. Line a baking sheet with parchment paper and set it aside.
2. In a dry skillet over medium heat, toast the pistachios for 34 minutes, stirring frequently, until fragrant and lightly browned. Remove from heat and set aside.
3. In a saucepan, combine powdered erythritol, unsalted butter, water, vanilla extract, and a pinch of salt (if using).
4. Cook the mixture over medium heat, stirring constantly, until the erythritol is dissolved and the mixture begins to bubble.
5. Once the mixture reaches a boil, add the baking soda and stir quickly. The mixture will foam up.
6. Immediately remove the saucepan from the heat and stir in the toasted pistachios until evenly coated.
7. Pour the pistachio mixture onto the prepared baking sheet and spread it out into an even layer using a spatula.
8. Let the brittle cool at room temperature for 1015 minutes, then transfer it to the refrigerator to chill for at least 1 hour or until firm.
9. Once chilled, break the brittle into pieces.
10. Store the pistachio brittle in an airtight container at room temperature for up to 1 week.

Nutritional Info (per serving about 2 pieces): Calories: 130 | Fat: 11g | Carbs: 4g | Protein: 3g

Prep: 15 mins | Bake: 20 mins | Serves: 12 brownies

Ingredients:

- 1/2 cup unsalted butter (113g)
- 1/2 cup powdered erythritol (100g)
- 2 large eggs
- 1 teaspoon vanilla extract (5ml)
- 1/2 cup almond flour (60g)
- 1/4 cup unsweetened cocoa powder (25g)
- 1/2 teaspoon baking powder (2.5g)
- Pinch of salt (optional)
- 1/2 cup chopped walnuts (60g)

Instructions:

1. Preheat your oven to 350°F (175°C) and grease or line an 8x8inch baking pan with parchment paper.
2. In a microwavesafe bowl, melt the unsalted butter in the microwave.
3. Stir in powdered erythritol until well combined.
4. Add the eggs and vanilla extract to the butter mixture, and mix until smooth.
5. In a separate bowl, whisk together almond flour, unsweetened cocoa powder, baking powder, and a pinch of salt (if using).
6. Gradually add the dry ingredients to the wet ingredients, stirring until just combined.
7. Fold in chopped walnuts until evenly distributed throughout the batter.
8. Pour the batter into the prepared baking pan and spread it out evenly.
9. Bake in the preheated oven for 2025 minutes or until a toothpick inserted into the center comes out with moist crumbs.
10. Remove from the oven and let the brownies cool completely in the pan before slicing into squares.
11. Serve and enjoy these delicious keto walnut brownies as a guiltfree treat!

Nutritional Info (per brownie): Calories: 150 | Fat: 14g | Carbs: 3g | Protein: 3g

SUGARFREE MACADAMIA NUT COOKIES

Prep: 15 mins | Bake: 12 mins | Makes: 18 cookies

Ingredients:

- 1 cup macadamia nut flour (120g)
- 1/4 cup powdered erythritol (50g)
- 1/4 cup unsalted butter, softened (57g)
- 1 large egg
- 1/2 teaspoon vanilla extract (2.5ml)
- Pinch of salt (optional)
- 1/4 cup chopped macadamia nuts (30g), for texture (optional)

Instructions:

1. Preheat your oven to 350°F (175°C) and line a baking sheet with parchment paper.
2. In a mixing bowl, cream together powdered erythritol and softened unsalted butter until smooth.
3. Add the egg and vanilla extract to the butter mixture, and beat until well combined.
4. Stir in macadamia nut flour and a pinch of salt (if using) until a dough forms.
5. Fold in chopped macadamia nuts, if desired, for added texture and flavor.
6. Scoop tablespoonsized portions of dough onto the prepared baking sheet, spacing them apart.
7. Use your hands or the back of a spoon to flatten each cookie slightly.
8. Bake in the preheated oven for 1012 minutes or until the edges are golden brown.
9. Remove from the oven and let the cookies cool on the baking sheet for 5 minutes.
10. Transfer the cookies to a wire rack to cool completely before serving.

Nutritional Info (per cookie): Calories: 100 | Fat: 10g | Carbs: 2g | Protein: 1g

ALMOND FLOUR CAKE

Prep: 15 mins | Bake: 30 mins | Serves: 8

Ingredients:

- 2 cups almond flour (200g)
- 1/2 cup powdered erythritol (100g)
- 1 teaspoon baking powder (5g)
- 1/4 teaspoon salt (1.25g)
- 1/2 cup unsalted butter, melted (113g)
- 4 large eggs
- 1/4 cup unsweetened almond milk (60ml)
- 1 teaspoon vanilla extract (5ml)

Instructions:

1. Preheat your oven to 350°F (175°C) and grease or line a 9inch round cake pan with parchment paper.
2. In a large mixing bowl, whisk together almond flour, powdered erythritol, baking powder, and salt until well combined.
3. In a separate bowl, whisk together melted unsalted butter, eggs, unsweetened almond milk, and vanilla extract until smooth.
4. Gradually pour the wet ingredients into the dry ingredients, stirring until just combined and no lumps remain.
5. Pour the batter into the prepared cake pan and spread it out evenly.
6. Bake in the preheated oven for 2530 minutes or until a toothpick inserted into the center comes out clean.
7. Remove from the oven and let the cake cool in the pan for 10 minutes.
8. Carefully transfer the cake to a wire rack to cool completely before slicing and serving.
9. Enjoy a slice of this delicious almond flour cake as a satisfying dessert or snack!

Nutritional Info (per serving): Calories: 280 | Fat: 24g | Carbs: 6g | Protein: 9g

Prep: 15 mins | Chill: 30 mins | Makes: 12 servings

Ingredients:

- 1/2 cup sugarfree peanut butter (120g)
- 2 tablespoons powdered erythritol (30g)
- 1/4 cup coconut oil, melted (60ml)
- 1/4 cup unsweetened cocoa powder (25g)
- 2 tablespoons powdered erythritol (30g)
- 1/2 teaspoon vanilla extract (2.5ml)
- Pinch of salt (optional)

Instructions:

1. In a mixing bowl, combine the sugarfree peanut butter and 2 tablespoons of powdered erythritol until smooth.
2. In a separate bowl, mix together the melted coconut oil, unsweetened cocoa powder, remaining 2 tablespoons of powdered erythritol, vanilla extract, and a pinch of salt (if using) until well combined.
3. Line a mini muffin tin with paper liners.
4. Spoon a small amount of the chocolate mixture into each paper liner, covering the bottom.
5. Place the muffin tin in the freezer for 10 minutes to set the chocolate layer.
6. Remove the muffin tin from the freezer and spoon a small amount of the peanut butter mixture on top of the chocolate layer in each paper liner.
7. Place the muffin tin back in the freezer for another 10 minutes to set the peanut butter layer.
8. Finally, spoon the remaining chocolate mixture over the peanut butter layer in each paper liner, covering completely.
9. Return the muffin tin to the freezer for a final 10 minutes to set the top chocolate layer.
10. Once set, remove the peanut butter cups from the muffin tin and store them in an airtight container in the refrigerator.
11. Enjoy these homemade lowcarb peanut butter cups as a guiltfree treat!

Nutritional Info (per serving 1 peanut butter cup): Calories: 120 | Fat: 11g | Carbs: 3g | Protein: 3g

KETO SEED CRACKERS

Prep: 10 mins | Bake: 30 mins | Serves: 12 servings

Ingredients:

- 1/2 cup flaxseeds (60g)
- 1/4 cup chia seeds (40g)
- 1/4 cup sesame seeds (40g)
- 1/4 cup sunflower seeds (40g)
- 1/4 cup pumpkin seeds (40g)
- 1/2 teaspoon salt (2.5g)
- 1/2 teaspoon garlic powder (2.5g)
- 1/2 teaspoon onion powder (2.5g)
- 1/4 cup water (60ml)

Instructions:

1. Preheat your oven to 325°F (160°C) and line a baking sheet with parchment paper.
2. In a mixing bowl, combine flaxseeds, chia seeds, sesame seeds, sunflower seeds, pumpkin seeds, salt, garlic powder, and onion powder. Mix well.
3. Add water to the seed mixture and stir until everything is evenly coated and starts to come together.
4. Transfer the mixture onto the prepared baking sheet and spread it out evenly.
5. Place another sheet of parchment paper on top of the seed mixture and use a rolling pin to flatten it into a thin, even layer.
6. Remove the top layer of parchment paper and use a knife or pizza cutter to score the mixture into crackers.
7. Bake in the preheated oven for 2530 minutes or until the crackers are golden brown and crisp.
8. Remove from the oven and let the crackers cool on the baking sheet for 10 minutes.
9. Break the crackers along the scored lines and let them cool completely on a wire rack.
10. Once cooled, store the keto seed crackers in an airtight container at room temperature for up to 1 week.

Nutritional Info (per serving about 2 crackers): Calories: 90 | Fat: 7g | Carbs: 3g | Protein: 3g

Prep: 10 mins | Chill: 1 hour | Serves: 8

Ingredients:

- 1 cup unsweetened almond butter (240g)
- 1/4 cup coconut oil, melted (60ml)
- 2 tablespoons powdered erythritol (30g)
- 1/2 teaspoon vanilla extract (2.5ml)
- Pinch of salt (optional)
- 2 ounces sugarfree dark chocolate, chopped (60g)
- 1/4 cup chopped almonds (30g)

Instructions:

1. Line a baking sheet with parchment paper and set it aside.
2. In a microwavesafe bowl, combine unsweetened almond butter, melted coconut oil, powdered erythritol, vanilla extract, and a pinch of salt (if using). Microwave in 30second intervals, stirring between each interval, until the mixture is smooth and well combined.
3. Pour the almond mixture onto the prepared baking sheet and spread it out into an even layer.
4. In a separate microwavesafe bowl, melt the sugarfree dark chocolate in 30second intervals, stirring between each interval, until smooth.
5. Drizzle the melted chocolate over the almond mixture on the baking sheet.
6. Use a knife or toothpick to swirl the chocolate into the almond mixture.
7. Sprinkle chopped almonds over the top of the almond bark.
8. Place the baking sheet in the refrigerator for at least 1 hour or until the almond bark is set.
9. Once set, break the almond bark into pieces and serve.
10. Store any leftovers in an airtight container in the refrigerator.

Nutritional Info (per serving about 2 pieces): Calories: 200 | Fat: 18g | Carbs: 5g | Protein: 5g

KETO ICE CREAM

Prep: 10 mins | Churn: 25 mins | Freeze: 4 hours | Serves: 4

Ingredients:

- 2 cups heavy cream (480ml)
- 1 cup unsweetened almond milk (240ml)
- 1/2 cup powdered erythritol (100g)
- 1 teaspoon vanilla extract (5ml)
- Pinch of salt (optional)

Instructions:

1. In a mixing bowl, combine heavy cream, unsweetened almond milk, powdered erythritol, vanilla extract, and a pinch of salt (if using). Mix well until the erythritol is dissolved.
2. Pour the mixture into an ice cream maker.
3. Churn according to the manufacturer's instructions until the ice cream reaches a softserve consistency.
4. Transfer the churned ice cream into a freezersafe container.
5. Cover the container and freeze the ice cream for at least 4 hours or until firm.
6. Once frozen, scoop and serve the keto ice cream.
7. Enjoy your creamy and indulgent treat without worrying about the sugar content!

Nutritional Info (per serving): Calories: 380 | Fat: 40g | Carbs: 3g | Protein: 2g

LOWCARB POPSICLES

Prep: 10 mins | Freeze: 4 hours | Serves: 6

Ingredients:

- 2 cups unsweetened coconut milk (480ml)
- 1/2 cup powdered erythritol (100g)
- 1 teaspoon vanilla extract (5ml)
- 1 cup mixed berries (150g)

Instructions:

1. In a blender, combine unsweetened coconut milk, powdered erythritol, and vanilla extract. Blend until smooth.
2. Place a few mixed berries into each popsicle mold.
3. Pour the coconut milk mixture into the molds, covering the berries.
4. Insert popsicle sticks into the molds.
5. Freeze the popsicles for at least 4 hours or until solid.
6. Once frozen, run the molds under warm water for a few seconds to release the popsicles.
7. Serve these refreshing lowcarb popsicles on a hot day as a guiltfree treat!

Nutritional Info (per serving): Calories: 90 | Fat: 8g | Carbs: 4g | Protein: 1g

SUGARFREE FROZEN YOGURT

Prep: 10 mins | Freeze: 4 hours | Serves: 4

Ingredients:

- 2 cups plain Greek yogurt (480g)
- 1/4 cup powdered erythritol (50g)
- 1 teaspoon vanilla extract (5ml)
- 1 cup diced strawberries (150g)

Instructions:

1. In a mixing bowl, combine plain Greek yogurt, powdered erythritol, and vanilla extract. Mix until well incorporated.
2. Gently fold in the diced strawberries.
3. Pour the mixture into a freezersafe container.
4. Cover the container and freeze the yogurt for at least 4 hours or until solid.
5. Once frozen, scoop the sugarfree frozen yogurt into bowls.
6. Enjoy the creamy texture and tangy flavor of this delightful dessert without the guilt!

Nutritional Info (per serving): Calories: 80 | Fat: 0g | Carbs: 8g | Protein: 14g

KETO MILKSHAKES

Prep: 5 mins | Serves: 2
Ingredients:

- 2 cups unsweetened almond milk (480ml)
- 1/2 cup heavy cream (120ml)
- 1/4 cup powdered erythritol (50g)
- 2 tablespoons unsweetened cocoa powder (10g)
- 1 teaspoon vanilla extract (5ml)
- 2 cups ice cubes

Instructions:

1. In a blender, combine unsweetened almond milk, heavy cream, powdered erythritol, unsweetened cocoa powder, vanilla extract, and ice cubes.
2. Blend on high speed until smooth and creamy.
3. Pour the keto milkshake into glasses and serve immediately.
4. Indulge in the rich and satisfying taste of this lowcarb milkshake without the added sugar!

Nutritional Info (per serving): Calories: 250 | Fat: 23g | Carbs: 6g | Protein: 2g

LOWCARB SORBET

Prep: 10 mins | Chill: 4 hours | Serves: 4
Ingredients:

- 2 cups frozen mixed berries (300g)
- 1/4 cup powdered erythritol (50g)
- 1 tablespoon fresh lemon juice (15ml)
- 1/4 cup water (60ml)

Instructions:

1. In a blender, combine frozen mixed berries, powdered erythritol, fresh lemon juice, and water.
2. Blend until smooth, scraping down the sides of the blender as needed.
3. Pour the mixture into a shallow dish or baking pan.
4. Cover the dish with plastic wrap and freeze for at least 4 hours or until firm.
5. Once frozen, use a fork to scrape and fluff the sorbet to create a light, icy texture.
6. Serve the lowcarb sorbet in bowls and enjoy its refreshing taste without the added sugars!

Nutritional Info (per serving): Calories: 50 | Fat: 0g | Carbs: 12g | Protein: 1g

SUGARFREE FROSTY

Prep: 5 mins | Serves: 2

Ingredients:

- 2 cups unsweetened almond milk (480ml)
- 1/2 cup heavy cream (120ml)
- 1/4 cup powdered erythritol (50g)
- 1 teaspoon vanilla extract (5ml)
- 2 cups ice cubes

Instructions:

1. In a blender, combine unsweetened almond milk, heavy cream, powdered erythritol, vanilla extract, and ice cubes.
2. Blend on high speed until smooth and creamy.
3. Pour the sugarfree frosty into glasses and serve immediately.
4. Enjoy the frosty texture and delicious flavor of this lowcarb frozen treat without worrying about added sugars!

Nutritional Info (per serving): Calories: 250 | Fat: 23g | Carbs: 6g | Protein: 2g

KETO ICE CREAM SANDWICHES

Prep: 20 mins | Chill: 4 hours | Serves: 6

Ingredients:

- 1 batch of keto cookies (such as almond flour cookies or coconut flour cookies)
- 2 cups keto ice cream (from the recipe provided or storebought)

Instructions:

1. Prepare a batch of keto cookies according to your chosen recipe. Let them cool completely.
2. Once the cookies have cooled, scoop a generous amount of keto ice cream onto the bottom side of one cookie.
3. Place another cookie on top of the ice cream to form a sandwich.
4. Gently press down on the top cookie to spread the ice cream to the edges.
5. Repeat with the remaining cookies and ice cream to make additional sandwiches.
6. Place the assembled ice cream sandwiches on a baking sheet lined with parchment paper.
7. Freeze the sandwiches for at least 4 hours or until firm.
8. Once frozen, wrap each ice cream sandwich individually in plastic wrap or foil.
9. Store the wrapped sandwiches in a freezersafe container until ready to serve.
10. Enjoy these delightful keto ice cream sandwiches as a cool and satisfying treat!

Nutritional Info (per serving): Nutritional info will vary based on the specific cookie and ice cream recipes used.

FROZEN CHEESECAKE

Prep: 20 mins | Chill: 4 hours | Serves: 8

Ingredients:

- 1 1/2 cups almond flour (180g)
- 1/4 cup powdered erythritol (50g)
- 1/4 cup unsalted butter, melted (57g)
- 16 ounces cream cheese, softened (450g)
- 1/2 cup powdered erythritol (100g)
- 1 teaspoon vanilla extract (5ml)
- 1 cup heavy cream (240ml)

Instructions:

1. In a mixing bowl, combine almond flour, powdered erythritol, and melted unsalted butter. Mix until well combined and crumbly.
2. Press the mixture into the bottom of a 9inch springform pan to form the crust. Place in the freezer to chill while preparing the filling.
3. In a separate mixing bowl, beat softened cream cheese, powdered erythritol, and vanilla extract until smooth and creamy.
4. In another mixing bowl, whip heavy cream until stiff peaks form.
5. Gently fold the whipped cream into the cream cheese mixture until evenly combined.
6. Pour the filling over the chilled crust in the springform pan, spreading it out evenly.
7. Place the pan in the freezer and chill for at least 4 hours or until firm.
8. Once frozen, remove the cheesecake from the freezer and let it sit at room temperature for a few minutes before slicing and serving.
9. Enjoy a slice of this creamy and indulgent lowcarb frozen cheesecake as a delightful dessert!

Nutritional Info (per serving): Calories: 300 | Fat: 28g | Carbs: 6g | Protein: 7g

SUGARFREE FROZEN CUSTARD

Prep: 15 mins | Churn: 25 mins | Chill: 4 hours | Serves: 6

Ingredients:

- 2 cups heavy cream (480ml)
- 1 cup unsweetened almond milk (240ml)
- 1/2 cup powdered erythritol (100g)
- 4 large egg yolks
- 1 teaspoon vanilla extract (5ml)

Instructions:

1. In a saucepan, heat heavy cream, unsweetened almond milk, and powdered erythritol over medium heat until it just begins to simmer. Do not boil.
2. In a mixing bowl, whisk egg yolks until smooth.
3. Gradually pour the hot cream mixture into the egg yolks, whisking constantly to prevent curdling.
4. Return the mixture to the saucepan and cook over low heat, stirring constantly, until it thickens enough to coat the back of a spoon.
5. Remove the custard from the heat and stir in vanilla extract.
6. Strain the custard through a finemesh sieve into a clean bowl to remove any lumps.
7. Cover the bowl with plastic wrap, pressing it directly onto the surface of the custard to prevent a skin from forming.
8. Chill the custard in the refrigerator for at least 4 hours or until completely cold.
9. Once chilled, pour the custard into an ice cream maker and churn according to the manufacturer's instructions until thick and creamy.
10. Transfer the churned custard into a freezersafe container and freeze for an additional 2 hours to firm up.
11. Serve the sugarfree frozen custard in bowls and enjoy its rich and creamy texture without the added sugars!

Nutritional Info (per serving): Calories: 350 | Fat: 33g | Carbs: 4g | Protein: 5g

KETO FROZEN YOGURT BITES

Prep: 10 mins | Freeze: 2 hours | Serves: 4

Ingredients:

- 1 cup plain Greek yogurt (240g)
- 1 tablespoon powdered erythritol (15g)
- 1/2 teaspoon vanilla extract (2.5ml)
- 1/2 cup mixed berries, chopped (75g)

Instructions:

1. In a mixing bowl, combine plain Greek yogurt, powdered erythritol, and vanilla extract. Mix until well combined.
2. Gently fold in the chopped mixed berries.
3. Line a mini muffin tin with paper liners.
4. Spoon the yogurt mixture into the prepared muffin tin, filling each cup about halfway.
5. Smooth the tops with the back of a spoon.
6. Place the muffin tin in the freezer and freeze for at least 2 hours or until firm.
7. Once frozen, remove the yogurt bites from the muffin tin.
8. Serve immediately or transfer to a freezersafe container and store in the freezer until ready to enjoy.
9. These keto frozen yogurt bites make a refreshing and guiltfree snack or dessert option!

Nutritional Info (per serving): Calories: 50 | Fat: 0g | Carbs: 5g | Protein: 6g

LOWCARB FROZEN FRUIT BARS

Prep: 10 mins | Freeze: 4 hours | Serves: 6

Ingredients:

- 2 cups mixed berries (300g)
- 1/4 cup powdered erythritol (50g)
- 1 tablespoon fresh lemon juice (15ml)
- 1/4 cup water (60ml)

Instructions:

1. In a blender, combine mixed berries, powdered erythritol, fresh lemon juice, and water.
2. Blend until smooth, scraping down the sides of the blender as needed.
3. Pour the mixture into popsicle molds.
4. Insert popsicle sticks into the molds.
5. Freeze the fruit bars for at least 4 hours or until solid.
6. Once frozen, run the molds under warm water for a few seconds to release the fruit bars.
7. Serve these refreshing lowcarb frozen fruit bars on a hot day as a guilt free treat!

Nutritional Info (per serving): Calories: 40 | Fat: 0g | Carbs: 9g | Protein: 1g

SUGARFREE FROZEN HOT CHOCOLATE

Prep: 10 mins | Freeze: 4 hours | Serves: 2

Ingredients:
- 2 cups unsweetened almond milk (480ml)
- 1/4 cup unsweetened cocoa powder (25g)
- 1/4 cup powdered erythritol (50g)
- 1/2 teaspoon vanilla extract (2.5ml)
- 2 cups ice cubes
- Sugarfree whipped cream, for topping (optional)

Instructions:
1. In a blender, combine unsweetened almond milk, unsweetened cocoa powder, powdered erythritol, vanilla extract, and ice cubes.
2. Blend on high speed until smooth and creamy.
3. Pour the sugarfree frozen hot chocolate into glasses.
4. Top with sugarfree whipped cream, if desired.
5. Serve immediately and enjoy this deliciously refreshing twist on a classic hot chocolate!

Nutritional Info (per serving): Calories: 50 | Fat: 4g | Carbs: 5g | Protein: 1g

KETO FROZEN MOUSSE

Prep: 10 mins | Chill: 4 hours | Serves: 4

Ingredients:
- 1 cup heavy cream (240ml)
- 1/4 cup powdered erythritol (50g)
- 2 tablespoons unsweetened cocoa powder (10g)
- 1 teaspoon vanilla extract (5ml)

Instructions:
1. In a mixing bowl, combine heavy cream, powdered erythritol, cocoa powder, and vanilla extract.
2. Using a hand mixer or stand mixer, beat the mixture on high speed until stiff peaks form.
3. Spoon the keto frozen mousse into serving glasses or ramekins.
4. Cover the glasses with plastic wrap and chill in the refrigerator for at least 4 hours or until set.
5. Once chilled, garnish with sugarfree whipped cream or a sprinkle of cocoa powder before serving.
6. Enjoy this light and airy keto frozen mousse as a delightful dessert option without the added sugars!

Nutritional Info (per serving): Calories: 200 | Fat: 21g | Carbs: 2g | Protein: 1g

LOWCARB FROZEN LEMONADE

Prep: 10 mins | Freeze: 4 hours | Serves: 4

Ingredients:
- 1 cup fresh lemon juice (240ml)
- 1/4 cup powdered erythritol (50g)
- 2 cups water (480ml)
- Lemon slices, for garnish (optional)
- Fresh mint leaves, for garnish (optional)

Instructions:
1. In a pitcher, combine fresh lemon juice, powdered erythritol, and water. Stir until the erythritol is dissolved.
2. Pour the lemonade mixture into popsicle molds.
3. Insert popsicle sticks into the molds.
4. Freeze the lemonade popsicles for at least 4 hours or until solid.
5. Once frozen, run the molds under warm water for a few seconds to release the popsicles.
6. Serve these refreshing lowcarb frozen lemonade popsicles on a hot day as a guiltfree treat!
7. Garnish with lemon slices and fresh mint leaves, if desired.

Nutritional Info (per serving): Calories: 15 | Fat: 0g | Carbs: 5g | Protein: 0g

SUGARFREE FROZEN PIE

Prep: 20 mins | Chill: 4 hours | Serves: 8

Ingredients:
- 1 prepared lowcarb pie crust (storebought or homemade)
- 2 cups heavy cream (480ml)
- 1/4 cup powdered erythritol (50g)
- 1 teaspoon vanilla extract (5ml)
- 1 cup sugarfree fruit preserves or pie filling (such as strawberry or blueberry)

Instructions:
1. Prepare a lowcarb pie crust and let it cool completely.
2. In a mixing bowl, combine heavy cream, powdered erythritol, and vanilla extract.
3. Using a hand mixer or stand mixer, beat the mixture on high speed until stiff peaks form.
4. Spread the sugarfree fruit preserves or pie filling evenly over the cooled pie crust.
5. Spoon the whipped cream mixture on top of the fruit layer, spreading it out evenly.
6. Cover the pie with plastic wrap and chill in the refrigerator for at least 4 hours or until set.
7. Once chilled, slice and serve the sugarfree frozen pie as a refreshing and satisfying dessert option without the added sugars!

Nutritional Info (per serving): Calories: 250 | Fat: 24g | Carbs: 4g | Protein: 2g

COCONUT FLOUR BROWNIES

Prep: 15 mins | Cook: 25 mins | Serves: 12

Ingredients:

- 1/2 cup coconut flour (60g)
- 1/2 cup cocoa powder (50g)
- 1/2 teaspoon baking powder
- 1/4 teaspoon salt
- 1/2 cup unsalted butter, melted (113g)
- 1/2 cup powdered erythritol (100g)
- 4 large eggs
- 1 teaspoon vanilla extract (5ml)
- 1/4 cup unsweetened almond milk (60ml)
- 1/4 cup chopped walnuts (30g) (optional)

Instructions:

1. Preheat your oven to 350°F (175°C) and grease a 9x9 inch baking pan.
2. In a mixing bowl, whisk together coconut flour, cocoa powder, baking powder, and salt.
3. In another bowl, mix melted butter and powdered erythritol until well combined.
4. Add eggs one at a time to the butter mixture, then stir in vanilla extract.
5. Gradually add dry ingredients to the wet mixture, alternating with almond milk, until well combined.
6. Fold in chopped walnuts, if using.
7. Pour the batter into the prepared baking pan and spread it out evenly.
8. Bake for 2025 minutes or until a toothpick inserted into the center comes out clean.
9. Allow the brownies to cool in the pan before slicing into squares.
10. Enjoy these moist and decadent coconut flour brownies guiltfree!

Nutritional Info (per serving): Calories: 140 | Fat: 11g | Carbs: 6g | Protein: 4g

ALMOND FLOUR CUPCAKES

Prep: 15 mins | Cook: 20 mins | Serves: 12

Ingredients:

- 2 cups almond flour (200g)
- 1/4 cup powdered erythritol (50g)
- 1/2 teaspoon baking powder
- 1/4 teaspoon salt
- 1/3 cup unsalted butter, melted (75g)
- 4 large eggs
- 1/4 cup unsweetened almond milk (60ml)
- 1 teaspoon vanilla extract (5ml)

Instructions:

1. Preheat your oven to 350°F (175°C) and line a muffin tin with cupcake liners.
2. In a mixing bowl, whisk together almond flour, powdered erythritol, baking powder, and salt.
3. In another bowl, mix melted butter, eggs, almond milk, and vanilla extract until well combined.
4. Gradually add dry ingredients to the wet mixture, stirring until smooth.
5. Spoon the batter into the prepared muffin tin, filling each cup about 2/3 full.
6. Bake for 1820 minutes or until a toothpick inserted into the center comes out clean.
7. Allow the cupcakes to cool in the tin for 5 minutes, then transfer them to a wire rack to cool completely.
8. Once cooled, frost the cupcakes with your favorite sugarfree frosting or enjoy them plain.
9. These almond flour cupcakes are moist, fluffy, and perfect for any occasion!

Nutritional Info (per serving): Calories: 180 | Fat: 15g | Carbs: 5g | Protein: 7g

Prep: 15 mins | Cook: 25 mins | Chill: 2 hours | Serves: 9

Ingredients:

- 1 cup almond flour (100g)
- 1/4 cup powdered erythritol (50g)
- 1/4 teaspoon salt
- 1/4 cup unsalted butter, melted (56g)
- 2 large eggs
- 1/4 cup fresh lemon juice (60ml)
- Zest of 1 lemon
- 1/4 cup powdered erythritol, for dusting (optional)

Instructions:

1. Preheat your oven to 350°F (175°C) and line an 8x8 inch baking dish with parchment paper.
2. In a mixing bowl, combine almond flour, powdered erythritol, salt, and melted butter until a dough forms.
3. Press the dough evenly into the bottom of the prepared baking dish.
4. Bake the crust for 1012 minutes or until lightly golden.
5. In another bowl, whisk together eggs, fresh lemon juice, and lemon zest until well combined.
6. Pour the lemon mixture over the baked crust and spread it out evenly.
7. Return the dish to the oven and bake for an additional 1215 minutes or until the filling is set.
8. Allow the lemon bars to cool completely in the dish, then refrigerate for at least 2 hours to chill.
9. Once chilled, dust the top of the bars with powdered erythritol, if desired, and slice into squares.
10. Enjoy these tangy and refreshing keto lemon bars as a delightful treat!

Nutritional Info (per serving): Calories: 130 | Fat: 11g | Carbs: 3g | Protein: 4g

Prep: 10 mins | Cook: 15 mins | Serves: 12

Ingredients:

- 2 cups unsweetened shredded coconut (160g)
- 1/3 cup powdered erythritol (65g)
- 2 large egg whites
- 1 teaspoon vanilla extract (5ml)
- Pinch of salt

Instructions:

1. Preheat your oven to 325°F (160°C) and line a baking sheet with parchment paper.
2. In a mixing bowl, combine shredded coconut and powdered erythritol.
3. In another bowl, whisk together egg whites, vanilla extract, and salt until frothy.
4. Pour the egg white mixture over the coconut mixture and stir until well combined.
5. Using a cookie scoop or your hands, shape the mixture into small mounds and place them onto the prepared baking sheet.
6. Bake the macaroons for 1215 minutes or until lightly golden around the edges.
7. Allow the macaroons to cool on the baking sheet for 5 minutes, then transfer them to a wire rack to cool completely.
8. Once cooled, store the lowcarb macaroons in an airtight container at room temperature.
9. Enjoy these chewy and coconutty treats as a guiltfree indulgence!

Nutritional Info (per serving): Calories: 70 | Fat: 6g | Carbs: 3g | Protein: 1g

GLUTENFREE CHEESECAKE

Prep: 20 mins | Bake: 50 mins | Chill: 4 hours | Serves: 8

Ingredients:

- 1 1/2 cups almond flour (150g)
- 1/4 cup powdered erythritol (50g)
- 1/4 teaspoon salt
- 1/4 cup unsalted butter, melted (56g)
- 16 oz cream cheese, softened (450g)
- 2/3 cup powdered erythritol (130g)
- 2 large eggs
- 1/4 cup sour cream (60ml)
- 1 teaspoon vanilla extract (5ml)
- Zest of 1 lemon

Instructions:

1. Preheat your oven to 325°F (160°C) and grease a 9inch springform pan.
2. In a mixing bowl, combine almond flour, powdered erythritol, salt, and melted butter until a crumbly mixture forms.
3. Press the mixture into the bottom of the prepared springform pan to form the crust.
4. In another bowl, beat cream cheese and powdered erythritol until smooth.
5. Add eggs, one at a time, mixing well after each addition.
6. Stir in sour cream, vanilla extract, and lemon zest until combined.
7. Pour the cheesecake filling over the crust in the pan and smooth out the top.
8. Bake for 5055 minutes or until the edges are set and the center is slightly jiggly.
9. Turn off the oven and let the cheesecake cool inside with the door slightly ajar for 1 hour.
10. Remove the cheesecake from the oven and refrigerate for at least 4 hours or until chilled and set.
11. Once chilled, slice the glutenfree cheesecake and serve with your favorite sugarfree toppings, if desired.
12. Enjoy this creamy and decadent dessert without worrying about gluten or excessive sugars!

Nutritional Info (per serving): Calories: 320 | Fat: 30g | Carbs: 6g | Protein: 9g

Prep: 20 mins | Chill: 4 hours | Serves: 8

Ingredients:

- 1 prepared lowcarb pie crust (storebought or homemade)
- 1 can fullfat coconut milk (400ml), chilled overnight
- 1/4 cup powdered erythritol (50g)
- 1 teaspoon vanilla extract (5ml)
- 1/2 cup unsweetened shredded coconut (40g), toasted
- Sugarfree whipped cream, for topping (optional)

Instructions:

1. Prepare a lowcarb pie crust and let it cool completely.
2. In a mixing bowl, scoop out the solid coconut cream from the chilled can of coconut milk, leaving behind the liquid.
3. Beat the coconut cream with powdered erythritol and vanilla extract until smooth and creamy.
4. Fold in toasted shredded coconut until evenly distributed.
5. Spoon the coconut cream mixture into the prepared pie crust and spread it out evenly.
6. Cover the pie with plastic wrap and refrigerate for at least 4 hours or until set.
7. Once chilled, top the keto coconut cream pie with sugarfree whipped cream, if desired.
8. Slice and serve this luscious coconut cream pie as a delightful ending to any meal!

Nutritional Info (per serving): Calories: 250 | Fat: 24g | Carbs: 6g | Protein: 3g

Prep: 15 mins | Cook: 2 hours | Serves: 12

Ingredients:

- 3 large egg whites
- 1/4 teaspoon cream of tartar
- 1/2 cup powdered erythritol (100g)
- 1 teaspoon vanilla extract (5ml)
- Pinch of salt

Instructions:

1. Preheat your oven to 200°F (95°C) and line a baking sheet with parchment paper.
2. In a clean, dry mixing bowl, beat egg whites and cream of tartar with an electric mixer until foamy.
3. Gradually add powdered erythritol, one tablespoon at a time, while continuing to beat the egg whites.
4. Beat the egg whites until stiff, glossy peaks form.
5. Fold in vanilla extract and a pinch of salt until evenly incorporated.
6. Drop spoonfuls of the meringue mixture onto the prepared baking sheet, spacing them apart.
7. Bake the meringue cookies in the preheated oven for 1.5 to 2 hours, or until they are dry and crisp on the outside.
8. Turn off the oven and let the meringue cookies cool completely inside with the door closed.
9. Once cooled, store the lowcarb meringue cookies in an airtight container at room temperature.
10. Enjoy these light and airy treats as a guiltfree snack or dessert option!

Nutritional Info (per serving): Calories: 10 | Fat: 0g | Carbs: 2g | Protein: 1g

SUGARFREE COCONUT PANNA COTTA

Prep: 10 mins | Chill: 4 hours | Serves: 4

Ingredients:

- 1 can full fat coconut milk (400ml)
- 1/4 cup powdered erythritol (50g)
- 1 teaspoon vanilla extract (5ml)
- 1 packet unflavored gelatin (7g)
- 2 tablespoons cold water (30ml)
- Unsweetened shredded coconut, for garnish (optional)

Instructions:

1. In a small bowl, sprinkle gelatin over cold water and let it bloom for 5 minutes.
2. In a saucepan, heat coconut milk and powdered erythritol over medium heat until steaming but not boiling.
3. Remove the saucepan from heat and stir in vanilla extract.
4. Add the bloomed gelatin to the coconut milk mixture and whisk until completely dissolved.
5. Divide the mixture evenly among four serving cups or ramekins.
6. Chill the coconut panna cotta in the refrigerator for at least 4 hours or until set.
7. Once set, garnish with unsweetened shredded coconut, if desired, before serving.
8. Enjoy this creamy and indulgent sugarfree coconut panna cotta as a satisfying dessert!

Nutritional Info (per serving): Calories: 200 | Fat: 18g | Carbs: 3g | Protein: 2g

KETO ALMOND FLOUR CAKE

Prep: 15 mins | Bake: 30 mins | Serves: 8

Ingredients:

- 2 cups almond flour (200g)
- 1/3 cup powdered erythritol (65g)
- 1 teaspoon baking powder
- 1/4 teaspoon salt
- 1/4 cup unsalted butter, melted (56g)
- 3 large eggs
- 1/4 cup unsweetened almond milk (60ml)
- 1 teaspoon vanilla extract (5ml)

Instructions:

1. Preheat your oven to 350°F (175°C) and grease an 8inch round cake pan.
2. In a mixing bowl, whisk together almond flour, powdered erythritol, baking powder, and salt.
3. In another bowl, mix melted butter, eggs, almond milk, and vanilla extract until well combined.
4. Gradually add dry ingredients to the wet mixture, stirring until smooth.
5. Pour the batter into the prepared cake pan and spread it out evenly.
6. Bake for 2530 minutes or until a toothpick inserted into the center comes out clean.
7. Allow the almond flour cake to cool in the pan for 10 minutes, then transfer it to a wire rack to cool completely.
8. Once cooled, slice and serve this moist and tender keto almond flour cake as a delightful dessert option!

Nutritional Info (per serving): Calories: 230 | Fat: 20g | Carbs: 5g | Protein: 7g

Prep: 5 mins (+ 2 hours chilling) | Serves: 4

Ingredients:

- 1 can fullfat coconut milk (400ml)
- 1/4 cup chia seeds (40g)
- 2 tablespoons powdered erythritol (30g)
- 1 teaspoon vanilla extract (5ml)
- Unsweetened shredded coconut, for garnish (optional)
- Berries, for topping (optional)

Instructions:

1. In a mixing bowl, whisk together coconut milk, chia seeds, powdered erythritol, and vanilla extract until well combined.
2. Let the mixture sit for 5 minutes, then whisk again to prevent clumping.
3. Cover the bowl and refrigerate the chia pudding for at least 2 hours or until thickened.
4. Once chilled and thickened, give the pudding a final stir before serving.
5. Divide the coconut chia pudding among four serving cups or bowls.
6. Garnish with unsweetened shredded coconut and fresh berries, if desired.
7. Enjoy this creamy and satisfying lowcarb coconut chia pudding as a nutritious breakfast or dessert!

Nutritional Info (per serving): Calories: 220 | Fat: 18g | Carbs: 8g | Protein: 4g

GLUTENFREE KETO BREAD PUDDING

Prep: 15 mins | Bake: 45 mins | Serves: 6

Ingredients:

- 4 cups cubed lowcarb bread (about 200g)
- 1 1/2 cups unsweetened almond milk (360ml)
- 4 large eggs
- 1/4 cup powdered erythritol (50g)
- 1 teaspoon vanilla extract (5ml)
- 1/2 teaspoon ground cinnamon
- Pinch of salt
- Sugarfree caramel sauce, for serving (optional)

Instructions:

1. Preheat your oven to 350°F (175°C) and grease a baking dish.
2. Spread the cubed lowcarb bread evenly in the prepared baking dish.
3. In a mixing bowl, whisk together almond milk, eggs, powdered erythritol, vanilla extract, cinnamon, and salt until well combined.
4. Pour the egg mixture over the cubed bread, making sure to coat all the pieces.
5. Let the bread pudding sit for 10 minutes to allow the bread to absorb the liquid.
6. Bake the bread pudding in the preheated oven for 4045 minutes or until set and golden brown on top.
7. Remove the bread pudding from the oven and let it cool slightly before serving.
8. Drizzle with sugarfree caramel sauce, if desired, before serving.
9. Enjoy this warm and comforting gluten free keto bread pudding as a cozy dessert treat!

Nutritional Info (per serving): Calories: 180 | Fat: 12g | Carbs: 6g | Protein: 10g

SUGARFREE COCONUT MACAROONS

Prep: 10 mins | Bake: 20 mins | Serves: 12

Ingredients:

- 3 cups unsweetened shredded coconut (240g)
- 1/3 cup powdered erythritol (65g)
- 3 large egg whites
- 1 teaspoon vanilla extract (5ml)
- Pinch of salt

Instructions:

1. Preheat your oven to 325°F (160°C) and line a baking sheet with parchment paper.
2. In a mixing bowl, combine shredded coconut and powdered erythritol.
3. In another bowl, beat egg whites, vanilla extract, and salt until stiff peaks form.
4. Gently fold the egg white mixture into the coconut mixture until well combined.
5. Using a spoon or cookie scoop, drop mounds of the coconut mixture onto the prepared baking sheet.
6. Bake the coconut macaroons in the preheated oven for 1820 minutes or until lightly golden.
7. Allow the macaroons to cool on the baking sheet for 5 minutes, then transfer them to a wire rack to cool completely.
8. Once cooled, store the sugarfree coconut macaroons in an airtight container at room temperature.
9. Enjoy these chewy and coconutty treats as a guilt free indulgence!

Nutritional Info (per serving): Calories: 90 | Fat: 8g | Carbs: 3g | Protein: 2g

Prep: 15 mins | Bake: 12 mins | Serves: 12

Ingredients:

- 2 cups almond flour (200g)
- 1/4 cup powdered erythritol (50g)
- 1/4 teaspoon baking soda
- 1/4 teaspoon salt
- 1/4 cup unsalted butter, melted (56g)
- 1 large egg
- 1 teaspoon vanilla extract (5ml)

Instructions:

1. Preheat your oven to 350°F (175°C) and line a baking sheet with parchment paper.
2. In a mixing bowl, whisk together almond flour, powdered erythritol, baking soda, and salt.
3. In another bowl, mix melted butter, egg, and vanilla extract until well combined.
4. Gradually add the dry ingredients to the wet mixture, stirring until a dough forms.
5. Scoop tablespoon sized portions of dough and roll them into balls.
6. Place the dough balls onto the prepared baking sheet and flatten them slightly with your fingers.
7. Bake the almond flour cookies in the preheated oven for 1012 minutes or until lightly golden around the edges.
8. Allow the cookies to cool on the baking sheet for 5 minutes, then transfer them to a wire rack to cool completely.
9. Once cooled, store the lowcarb almond flour cookies in an airtight container at room temperature.
10. Enjoy these soft and chewy cookies as a delightful treat!

Nutritional Info (per serving): Calories: 130 | Fat: 11g | Carbs: 3g | Protein: 4g

Prep: 15 mins | Chill: 2 hours | Serves: 4

Ingredients:

- 1 can full fat coconut milk (400ml), chilled overnight
- 1/4 cup powdered erythritol (50g)
- 1 teaspoon vanilla extract (5ml)
- 1/2 cup unsweetened shredded coconut (40g)
- Sugarfree chocolate shavings, for garnish (optional)
- Fresh berries, for garnish (optional)

Instructions:

1. Scoop out the solid coconut cream from the chilled can of coconut milk into a mixing bowl, leaving behind the liquid.
2. Add powdered erythritol and vanilla extract to the coconut cream and beat until smooth and creamy.
3. In serving glasses or jars, layer the coconut cream mixture with shredded coconut to create parfaits.
4. Repeat the layers until the glasses are filled, ending with a layer of coconut cream on top.
5. Cover the parfaits with plastic wrap and refrigerate for at least 2 hours to chill and set.
6. Once chilled, garnish the keto coconut cream parfaits with sugarfree chocolate shavings and fresh berries, if desired.
7. Serve and enjoy this indulgent and creamy dessert!

Nutritional Info (per serving): Calories: 250 | Fat: 23g | Carbs: 5g | Protein: 2g

GLUTENFREE KETO BISCOTTI

Prep: 15 mins | Bake: 45 mins | Serves: 12

Ingredients:

- 2 cups almond flour (200g)
- 1/3 cup powdered erythritol (65g)
- 1 teaspoon baking powder
- 1/4 teaspoon salt
- 2 large eggs
- 1 teaspoon vanilla extract (5ml)
- 1/4 cup unsweetened shredded coconut (20g)
- 1/4 cup sliced almonds (30g)

Instructions:

1. Preheat your oven to 325°F (160°C) and line a baking sheet with parchment paper.
2. In a mixing bowl, whisk together almond flour, powdered erythritol, baking powder, and salt.
3. In another bowl, beat eggs and vanilla extract until well combined.
4. Gradually add the dry ingredients to the egg mixture, stirring until a dough forms.
5. Fold in shredded coconut and sliced almonds until evenly distributed.
6. Transfer the dough onto the prepared baking sheet and shape it into a log about 12 inches long and 3 inches wide.
7. Bake the biscotti dough in the preheated oven for 2530 minutes or until firm and lightly golden.
8. Remove the biscotti log from the oven and let it cool for 10 minutes.
9. Reduce the oven temperature to 300°F (150°C).
10. Carefully slice the biscotti log into 1inch thick slices using a sharp knife.
11. 1Place the biscotti slices back onto the baking sheet and bake for an additional 15 minutes, flipping halfway through, until crisp and golden.
12. 1Allow the glutenfree keto biscotti to cool completely on a wire rack before serving.
13. Enjoy these crunchy and flavorful biscotti with a cup of your favorite sugarfree beverage!

Nutritional Info (per serving): Calories: 150 | Fat: 12g | Carbs: 4g | Protein: 6g

VEGAN KETO BROWNIES

Prep: 10 mins | Bake: 25 mins | Serves: 12

Ingredients:

- 1 cup almond flour (100g)
- 1/4 cup cocoa powder (20g)
- 1/4 cup powdered erythritol (50g)
- 1/4 teaspoon baking powder
- 1/4 teaspoon salt
- 1/2 cup unsweetened applesauce (120ml)
- 1/4 cup almond milk (60ml)
- 1/4 cup melted coconut oil (60ml)
- 1 teaspoon vanilla extract (5ml)

Instructions:

1. Preheat the oven to 350°F (175°C) and grease a baking dish.
2. In a mixing bowl, combine almond flour, cocoa powder, powdered erythritol, baking powder, and salt.
3. Add applesauce, almond milk, melted coconut oil, and vanilla extract to the dry ingredients.
4. Mix until well combined and pour the batter into the prepared baking dish.
5. Spread the batter evenly and bake for 25 minutes or until a toothpick inserted into the center comes out clean.
6. Allow the brownies to cool before slicing and serving.
7. Enjoy these indulgent vegan keto brownies as a guiltfree dessert!

Nutritional Info (per serving): Calories: 120 | Fat: 10g | Carbs: 5g | Protein: 3g

CHIA SEED PUDDING

Prep: 5 mins (+ 2 hours chilling) | Serves: 4

Ingredients:

- 1/4 cup chia seeds (40g)
- 1 cup unsweetened almond milk (240ml)
- 1 tablespoon powdered erythritol (15g)
- 1/2 teaspoon vanilla extract (3ml)

Instructions:

1. In a mixing bowl, combine chia seeds, almond milk, powdered erythritol, and vanilla extract.
2. Stir well to ensure the chia seeds are evenly distributed.
3. Cover the bowl and refrigerate for at least 2 hours or overnight, allowing the chia seeds to gel and thicken the pudding.
4. Once chilled, give the pudding a good stir before serving.
5. Divide the chia seed pudding into serving cups or bowls.
6. Serve chilled and enjoy this nutritious and satisfying dessert!

Nutritional Info (per serving): Calories: 70 | Fat: 4g | Carbs: 6g | Protein: 3g

VEGAN AVOCADO CHOCOLATE MOUSSE

Prep: 10 mins | Chill: 1 hour | Serves: 4

Ingredients:

- 2 ripe avocados
- 1/4 cup cocoa powder (20g)
- 1/4 cup powdered erythritol (50g)
- 1/4 cup unsweetened almond milk (60ml)
- 1 teaspoon vanilla extract (5ml)

Instructions:

1. Scoop the flesh of the avocados into a blender or food processor.
2. Add cocoa powder, powdered erythritol, almond milk, and vanilla extract.
3. Blend until smooth and creamy, scraping down the sides as needed.
4. Transfer the avocado chocolate mousse into serving cups or bowls.
5. Chill in the refrigerator for at least 1 hour to set.
6. Serve chilled and enjoy this rich and decadent vegan dessert!

Nutritional Info (per serving): Calories: 180 | Fat: 15g | Carbs: 10g | Protein: 3g

Prep: 10 mins (+ 4 hours chilling) | Serves: 4

Ingredients:

- 1 can full fat coconut milk (400ml), chilled overnight
- 1/4 cup powdered erythritol (50g)
- 1 teaspoon vanilla extract (5ml)
- Pinch of salt

Instructions:

1. Scoop out the solid coconut cream from the chilled can of coconut milk into a mixing bowl, leaving behind the liquid.
2. Add powdered erythritol, vanilla extract, and a pinch of salt to the coconut cream.
3. Using a hand mixer or whisk, beat the mixture until smooth and creamy.
4. Transfer the coconut cream mixture to an ice cream maker and churn according to the manufacturer's instructions.
5. Once churned, transfer the coconut milk ice cream to a freezersafe container and freeze for at least 4 hours or until firm.
6. Scoop and serve this creamy and dairyfree ice cream as a refreshing dessert treat!

Nutritional Info (per serving): Calories: 200 | Fat: 18g | Carbs: 6g | Protein: 2g

LOWCARB VEGAN CHEESECAKE

Prep: 20 mins (+ 4 hours chilling) | Serves: 8

Ingredients:

- 1 1/2 cups raw cashews, soaked in water for 4 hours or overnight
- 1/4 cup coconut oil, melted (60ml)
- 1/4 cup lemon juice (60ml)
- 1/4 cup powdered erythritol (50g)
- 1 teaspoon vanilla extract (5ml)
- 1/4 teaspoon salt
- 1 cup unsweetened almond milk (240ml)
- 1 tablespoon agar agar powder (7g)
- Fresh berries, for topping (optional)

Instructions:

1. Drain the soaked cashews and rinse under cold water.
2. In a blender, combine the soaked cashews, melted coconut oil, lemon juice, powdered erythritol, vanilla extract, and salt.
3. Blend until smooth and creamy, scraping down the sides as needed.
4. In a saucepan, heat almond milk over medium heat until warm but not boiling.
5. Whisk in agar agar powder and continue to cook, stirring constantly, for 23 minutes until the agar agar is fully dissolved.
6. Remove the saucepan from heat and let the mixture cool slightly.
7. Pour the cashew mixture into the saucepan with the agar agar mixture and whisk until well combined.
8. Pour the cheesecake mixture into a springform pan lined with parchment paper and smooth the top with a spatula.
9. Chill the cheesecake in the refrigerator for at least 4 hours or until set.
10. Once set, remove the cheesecake from the pan, slice, and serve with fresh berries, if desired.
11. Enjoy this decadent and creamy lowcarb vegan cheesecake as a delightful dessert!

Nutritional Info (per serving): Calories: 250 | Fat: 20g | Carbs: 9g | Protein: 6g

Prep: 20 mins (+ 1 hour chilling) | Serves: 12

Ingredients:

- 1/2 cup raw cashews (65g)
- 1/4 cup cocoa powder (20g)
- 1/4 cup powdered erythritol (50g)
- 2 tablespoons coconut oil, melted (30ml)
- 1/2 teaspoon vanilla extract (3ml)
- Unsweetened shredded coconut, for rolling (optional)
- Cocoa powder, for dusting (optional)

Instructions:

1. In a food processor, blend cashews until finely ground.
2. Add cocoa powder, powdered erythritol, melted coconut oil, and vanilla extract to the food processor.
3. Pulse until the mixture comes together and forms a dough.
4. Roll the dough into small balls and place them on a baking sheet lined with parchment paper.
5. Optional: Roll the truffles in unsweetened shredded coconut or dust with cocoa powder for added flavor and texture.
6. Chill the truffles in the refrigerator for at least 1 hour to firm up.
7. Once chilled, serve and enjoy these rich and indulgent sugarfree vegan truffles as a guilt free dessert!

Nutritional Info (per serving): Calories: 90 | Fat: 7g | Carbs: 4g | Protein: 2g

Prep: 10 mins | Bake: 20 mins | Serves: 12

Ingredients:

- 2 cups unsweetened shredded coconut (160g)
- 1/4 cup powdered erythritol (50g)
- 1/4 cup coconut flour (30g)
- 1/4 cup coconut oil, melted (60ml)
- 1/4 cup unsweetened almond milk (60ml)
- 1 teaspoon vanilla extract (5ml)
- Pinch of salt

Instructions:

1. Preheat your oven to 350°F (175°C) and line a baking sheet with parchment paper.
2. In a mixing bowl, combine shredded coconut, powdered erythritol, coconut flour, and a pinch of salt.
3. Add melted coconut oil, almond milk, and vanilla extract to the dry ingredients.
4. Mix until well combined and the mixture holds together.
5. Scoop tablespoonsized portions of the mixture and shape them into balls or small mounds.
6. Place the coconut macaroons onto the prepared baking sheet.
7. Bake in the preheated oven for 1820 minutes or until golden brown on the edges.
8. Allow the macaroons to cool on the baking sheet for a few minutes before transferring them to a wire rack to cool completely.
9. Serve and enjoy these delightful keto vegan coconut macaroons as a tasty dessert or snack!

Nutritional Info (per serving): Calories: 120 | Fat: 11g | Carbs: 4g | Protein: 1g

Prep: 5 mins | Cook: 10 mins | Serves: 8

Ingredients:

- 1/2 cup canned coconut milk (120ml)
- 1/4 cup powdered erythritol (50g)
- 2 tablespoons coconut oil (30ml)
- 1 teaspoon vanilla extract (5ml)
- Pinch of salt

Instructions:

1. In a saucepan over medium heat, combine coconut milk, powdered erythritol, coconut oil, vanilla extract, and a pinch of salt.
2. Bring the mixture to a gentle boil, then reduce the heat to low.
3. Simmer the sauce for 810 minutes, stirring frequently, until thickened and caramelized.
4. Remove the saucepan from the heat and let the caramel sauce cool slightly.
5. Transfer the caramel sauce to a glass jar or container for storage.
6. Serve warm or at room temperature over desserts like ice cream or cakes.
7. Store any leftover caramel sauce in the refrigerator for up to one week.

Nutritional Info (per serving): Calories: 80 | Fat: 8g | Carbs: 2g | Protein: 0g

Prep: 15 mins | Chill: 30 mins | Serves: 12

Ingredients:

- 1/2 cup creamy peanut butter (120g)
- 2 tablespoons coconut oil, melted (30ml)
- 1/4 cup powdered erythritol (50g)
- 1/4 teaspoon vanilla extract (1ml)
- 1/4 cup cocoa powder (20g)

Instructions:

1. In a mixing bowl, combine creamy peanut butter, melted coconut oil, powdered erythritol, and vanilla extract.
2. Stir until well combined and smooth.
3. Line a mini muffin tin with paper liners.
4. Spoon a small amount of the peanut butter mixture into each muffin cup, filling them about halfway.
5. Place the muffin tin in the freezer for 10 minutes to firm up the peanut butter layer.
6. In a separate bowl, mix cocoa powder with a tablespoon of melted coconut oil to create a chocolate mixture.
7. Remove the muffin tin from the freezer and spoon the chocolate mixture over the peanut butter layer in each cup.
8. Return the muffin tin to the freezer and chill for another 20 minutes until the chocolate layer is set.
9. Once set, remove the peanut butter cups from the muffin tin and store them in an airtight container in the refrigerator.
10. Enjoy these delicious vegan keto peanut butter cups as a satisfying sweet treat!

Nutritional Info (per serving): Calories: 120 | Fat: 11g | Carbs: 3g | Protein: 4g

SUGARFREE VEGAN FUDGE

Prep: 10 mins | Chill: 2 hours | Serves: 12

Ingredients:

- 1 cup raw cashews (130g)
- 1/4 cup coconut oil, melted (60ml)
- 1/4 cup cocoa powder (20g)
- 1/4 cup powdered erythritol (50g)
- 1 teaspoon vanilla extract (5ml)
- Pinch of salt

Instructions:

1. Place the raw cashews in a food processor and blend until finely ground.
2. Add melted coconut oil, cocoa powder, powdered erythritol, vanilla extract, and a pinch of salt to the food processor.
3. Process the mixture until it forms a smooth and thick paste.
4. Line a small baking dish with parchment paper, leaving some overhang on the sides for easy removal.
5. Transfer the fudge mixture into the lined baking dish and spread it out evenly with a spatula.
6. Place the baking dish in the refrigerator and chill the fudge for at least 2 hours or until firm.
7. Once set, lift the fudge out of the dish using the parchment paper and cut it into small squares.
8. Serve and enjoy this decadent sugarfree vegan fudge as a delightful treat!

Nutritional Info (per serving): Calories: 100 | Fat: 8g | Carbs: 4g | Protein: 3g

KETO VEGAN BREAD PUDDING

Prep: 15 mins | Bake: 45 mins | Serves: 8

Ingredients:

- 4 cups stale lowcarb bread, cubed (about 8 slices)
- 1 can fullfat coconut milk (400ml)
- 1/4 cup powdered erythritol (50g)
- 1 teaspoon vanilla extract (5ml)
- 1/2 teaspoon ground cinnamon
- Pinch of salt
- 1/4 cup chopped nuts (optional)
- Sugarfree caramel sauce, for serving (optional)

Instructions:

1. Preheat your oven to 350°F (175°C) and grease a baking dish.
2. Place the cubed lowcarb bread in the prepared baking dish.
3. In a mixing bowl, whisk together coconut milk, powdered erythritol, vanilla extract, ground cinnamon, and a pinch of salt.
4. Pour the coconut milk mixture over the cubed bread, ensuring that all pieces are evenly coated.
5. Let the bread soak in the coconut milk mixture for about 10 minutes, pressing down gently with a spatula to help the bread absorb the liquid.
6. Sprinkle chopped nuts over the bread pudding, if using.
7. Bake in the preheated oven for 4045 minutes, or until the top is golden brown and the pudding is set.
8. Remove the bread pudding from the oven and let it cool slightly before serving.
9. Drizzle with sugarfree caramel sauce, if desired, and enjoy this comforting keto vegan bread pudding!

Nutritional Info (per serving): Calories: 200 | Fat: 15g | Carbs: 10g | Protein: 5g

Prep: 30 mins | Bake: 15 mins | Chill: 1 hour | Serves: 6

Ingredients:

- 1 1/2 cups almond flour (180g)
- 1/4 cup coconut oil, melted (60ml)
- 2 tablespoons powdered erythritol (25g)
- 1/4 teaspoon almond extract (1ml)
- Pinch of salt
- 1/2 cup mixed fresh berries (such as strawberries, blueberries, and raspberries)
- Sugarfree fruit preserves or jam, for topping (optional)

Instructions:

1. Preheat your oven to 350°F (175°C) and grease a muffin tin.
2. In a mixing bowl, combine almond flour, melted coconut oil, powdered erythritol, almond extract, and a pinch of salt.
3. Mix until a dough forms and holds together.
4. Divide the dough into 6 equal portions and press each portion into the bottom and up the sides of the greased muffin tin to form tart shells.
5. Prick the bottom of each tart shell with a fork to prevent air bubbles from forming during baking.
6. Bake in the preheated oven for 1215 minutes, or until the tart shells are golden brown around the edges.
7. Remove the tart shells from the oven and let them cool completely in the muffin tin.
8. Once cooled, carefully remove the tart shells from the muffin tin and fill each shell with mixed fresh berries.
9. Optional: Heat sugarfree fruit preserves or jam in a small saucepan over low heat until melted, then drizzle over the filled tart shells for added flavor.
10. Chill the fruit tarts in the refrigerator for at least 1 hour before serving.
11. Enjoy these delightful lowcarb vegan fruit tarts as a refreshing dessert!

Nutritional Info (per serving): Calories: 250 | Fat: 20g | Carbs: 10g | Protein: 6g

Prep: 15 mins | Bake: 30 mins | Serves: 6

Ingredients:

- 1/2 cup almond flour (60g)
- 1/4 cup coconut flour (30g)
- 1/4 cup powdered erythritol (50g)
- 1/2 teaspoon baking powder (2.5g)
- Pinch of salt
- 1/4 cup coconut oil, melted (60ml)
- 1/2 cup unsweetened almond milk (120ml)
- 1 teaspoon vanilla extract (5ml)
- Vegan whipped cream, for filling
- Sugarfree chocolate sauce, for drizzling (optional)

Instructions:

1. Preheat your oven to 350°F (175°C) and line a baking sheet with parchment paper.
2. In a mixing bowl, whisk together almond flour, coconut flour, powdered erythritol, baking powder, and a pinch of salt.
3. Add melted coconut oil, unsweetened almond milk, and vanilla extract to the dry ingredients.
4. Stir until a thick batter forms and all ingredients are well combined.
5. Spoon the batter into 6 mounds on the prepared baking sheet, leaving space between each mound for spreading.
6. Use wet fingers to shape each mound into a round shape, smoothing out the tops.
7. Bake in the preheated oven for 2530 minutes, or until the cream puffs are golden brown and firm to the touch.
8. Remove the cream puffs from the oven and let them cool completely on the baking sheet.
9. Once cooled, slice each cream puff in half horizontally and fill with vegan whipped cream.
10. Optional: Drizzle sugarfree chocolate sauce over the filled cream puffs for extra indulgence.
11. Serve and enjoy these delightful vegan keto cream puffs as a decadent dessert!

Nutritional Info (per serving): Calories: 180 | Fat: 15g | Carbs: 6g | Protein: 3g

SUGARFREE VEGAN PUMPKIN PIE

Prep: 20 mins | Bake: 45 mins | Chill: 2 hours | Serves: 8

Ingredients:

- 1 1/2 cups canned pumpkin puree (360g)
- 1/2 cup canned coconut milk (120ml)
- 1/4 cup powdered erythritol (50g)
- 1 teaspoon ground cinnamon
- 1/2 teaspoon ground ginger
- 1/4 teaspoon ground nutmeg
- Pinch of salt
- 1 vegan pie crust (storebought or homemade)

Instructions:

1. Preheat your oven to 350°F (175°C).
2. In a mixing bowl, combine canned pumpkin puree, canned coconut milk, powdered erythritol, ground cinnamon, ground ginger, ground nutmeg, and a pinch of salt.
3. Mix until all ingredients are well combined and the filling is smooth.
4. Pour the pumpkin filling into the prepared vegan pie crust, spreading it out evenly.
5. Place the pie in the preheated oven and bake for 4550 minutes, or until the filling is set and the crust is golden brown.
6. Remove the pie from the oven and let it cool to room temperature.
7. Once cooled, transfer the pie to the refrigerator and chill for at least 2 hours before serving.
8. Slice and enjoy this delicious sugarfree vegan pumpkin pie as a festive dessert!

Nutritional Info (per serving): Calories: 180 | Fat: 12g | Carbs: 15g | Protein: 2g

LOWCARB VEGAN COCONUT BARS

Prep: 15 mins | Chill: 2 hours | Serves: 12

Ingredients:

- 1 cup unsweetened shredded coconut (80g)
- 1/4 cup coconut oil, melted (60ml)
- 1/4 cup powdered erythritol (50g)
- 1/4 cup almond flour (30g)
- 1/2 teaspoon vanilla extract (2.5ml)
- Pinch of salt
- Sugarfree chocolate chips, for drizzling (optional)

Instructions:

1. Line a baking dish with parchment paper, leaving some overhang on the sides for easy removal.
2. In a mixing bowl, combine unsweetened shredded coconut, melted coconut oil, powdered erythritol, almond flour, vanilla extract, and a pinch of salt.
3. Mix until all ingredients are well combined and the mixture holds together.
4. Press the coconut mixture evenly into the prepared baking dish.
5. Place the baking dish in the refrigerator and chill the coconut mixture for at least 2 hours or until firm.
6. Once chilled, remove the coconut mixture from the baking dish and cut it into bars.
7. Optional: Melt sugarfree chocolate chips in a microwavesafe bowl and drizzle over the coconut bars for extra flavor.
8. Return the coconut bars to the refrigerator for a few minutes to allow the chocolate to set.
9. Serve and enjoy these delicious lowcarb vegan coconut bars as a satisfying snack or dessert!

Nutritional Info (per serving): Calories: 120 | Fat: 10g | Carbs: 5g | Protein: 1g

FESTIVE LOWCARB PUMPKIN PIE

Prep: 15 mins | Bake: 50 mins | Serves: 8

Ingredients:

- 1 (9inch) unbaked lowcarb pie crust
- 1 can (15 ounces) pumpkin puree (425g)
- 1 cup unsweetened almond milk (240ml)
- 2 large eggs
- 1/2 cup powdered erythritol (100g)
- 1 teaspoon ground cinnamon
- 1/2 teaspoon ground ginger
- 1/4 teaspoon ground nutmeg
- 1/4 teaspoon salt
- Whipped cream, for serving (optional)

Instructions:

1. Preheat your oven to 425°F (220°C) and place the unbaked pie crust in a pie dish.
2. In a mixing bowl, whisk together pumpkin puree, unsweetened almond milk, eggs, powdered erythritol, ground cinnamon, ground ginger, ground nutmeg, and salt until smooth.
3. Pour the pumpkin mixture into the pie crust, spreading it out evenly.
4. Bake the pie in the preheated oven for 15 minutes.
5. After 15 minutes, reduce the oven temperature to 350°F (175°C) and continue baking for another 3540 minutes, or until the filling is set and a knife inserted into the center comes out clean.
6. Remove the pie from the oven and let it cool completely on a wire rack.
7. Once cooled, slice and serve the lowcarb pumpkin pie with whipped cream if desired.
8. Enjoy this festive treat with loved ones during the holiday season!

Nutritional Info (per serving): Calories: 150 | Fat: 10g | Carbs: 12g | Protein: 4g

Prep: 15 mins | Bake: 25 mins | Serves: 12

Ingredients:

- 1 1/2 cups almond flour (180g)
- 1/3 cup powdered erythritol (65g)
- 1/4 teaspoon salt
- 6 tablespoons unsalted butter, melted (85g)
- 2 large eggs
- 1/2 cup sugarfree maple syrup (120ml)
- 1 teaspoon vanilla extract (5ml)
- 1 1/2 cups chopped pecans (180g)

Instructions:

1. Preheat your oven to 350°F (175°C) and line an 8x8inch baking dish with parchment paper.
2. In a mixing bowl, combine almond flour, powdered erythritol, and salt.
3. Add melted butter to the dry ingredients and mix until well combined.
4. Press the mixture evenly into the bottom of the prepared baking dish to form the crust.
5. Bake the crust in the preheated oven for 10 minutes.
6. In another mixing bowl, whisk together eggs, sugarfree maple syrup, and vanilla extract.
7. Stir in chopped pecans until evenly coated.
8. Pour the pecan mixture over the partially baked crust, spreading it out evenly.
9. Return the baking dish to the oven and bake for an additional 15 minutes, or until the filling is set.
10. Remove from the oven and let it cool completely in the baking dish.
11. Once cooled, lift the pecan pie bars out of the dish using the parchment paper and cut into squares.
12. Serve and enjoy these delicious keto pecan pie bars as a holiday dessert!

Nutritional Info (per serving): Calories: 220 | Fat: 20g | Carbs: 6g | Protein: 5g

SUGARFREE GINGERBREAD COOKIES

Prep: 20 mins | Chill: 1 hour | Bake: 10 mins | Serves: 24

Ingredients:

- 2 cups almond flour (240g)
- 1/4 cup coconut flour (30g)
- 1 teaspoon ground ginger
- 1 teaspoon ground cinnamon
- 1/4 teaspoon ground nutmeg
- 1/4 teaspoon ground cloves
- 1/4 teaspoon baking soda
- 1/4 teaspoon salt
- 1/3 cup powdered erythritol (65g)
- 1/4 cup unsalted butter, softened (60g)
- 1/4 cup sugarfree maple syrup (60ml)
- 1 teaspoon vanilla extract (5ml)

Instructions:

1. In a mixing bowl, whisk together almond flour, coconut flour, ground ginger, ground cinnamon, ground nutmeg, ground cloves, baking soda, salt, and powdered erythritol.
2. Add softened butter, sugarfree maple syrup, and vanilla extract to the dry ingredients.
3. Mix until a dough forms, then knead the dough until smooth.
4. Wrap the dough in plastic wrap and chill in the refrigerator for at least 1 hour.
5. Preheat your oven to 350°F (175°C) and line a baking sheet with parchment paper.
6. Roll out the chilled dough on a lightly floured surface to about 1/4inch thickness.
7. Use cookie cutters to cut out shapes from the dough and place them on the prepared baking sheet.
8. Bake the cookies in the preheated oven for 810 minutes, or until lightly golden around the edges.
9. Remove from the oven and let the cookies cool on the baking sheet for a few minutes before transferring them to a wire rack to cool completely.
10. Once cooled, decorate the sugarfree gingerbread cookies as desired or enjoy them as is.
11. Store in an airtight container at room temperature for up to one week.

Nutritional Info (per serving 1 cookie): Calories: 70 | Fat: 6g | Carbs: 3g | Protein: 2g

Prep: 30 mins | Bake: 15 mins | Serves: 8

Ingredients:

- 4 large eggs, separated
- 1/2 cup powdered erythritol (100g)
- 1 teaspoon vanilla extract (5ml)
- 1/2 cup almond flour (60g)
- 2 tablespoons cocoa powder (unsweetened)
- 1/2 teaspoon baking powder (2.5g)
- 1/4 teaspoon salt
- 1 cup sugarfree whipped cream (240ml)
- Sugarfree chocolate shavings, for decoration (optional)

Instructions:

1. Preheat your oven to 350°F (175°C) and line a 10x15inch jelly roll pan with parchment paper.
2. In a mixing bowl, beat egg whites until stiff peaks form.
3. In another mixing bowl, beat egg yolks with powdered erythritol and vanilla extract until pale and creamy.
4. Gradually fold the beaten egg whites into the egg yolk mixture until well combined.
5. In a separate bowl, sift together almond flour, cocoa powder, baking powder, and salt.
6. Gently fold the dry ingredients into the egg mixture until no streaks remain.
7. Pour the batter into the prepared jelly roll pan and spread it out evenly.
8. Bake in the preheated oven for 1215 minutes, or until the cake is set and springs back when lightly touched.
9. Remove the cake from the oven and let it cool slightly in the pan.
10. Carefully transfer the cake onto a clean kitchen towel dusted with powdered erythritol.
11. Starting from one short end, roll up the cake and towel together into a log.
12. Let the rolled cake cool completely on a wire rack.
13. Once cooled, carefully unroll the cake and spread sugarfree whipped cream evenly over the surface.
14. Roll the cake back up without the towel and place it seamside down on a serving platter.
15. Decorate the yule log with sugarfree chocolate shavings if desired.
16. Slice and serve this festive lowcarb yule log as a delightful holiday dessert!

Nutritional Info (per serving): Calories: 130 | Fat: 10g | Carbs: 5g | Protein: 5g

Prep: 20 mins | Chill: 4 hours | Serves: 10

Ingredients:

- 1 1/2 cups almond flour (180g)
- 1/4 cup powdered erythritol (50g)
- 1/4 cup unsalted butter, melted (60g)
- 16 ounces cream cheese, softened (450g)
- 1/2 cup powdered erythritol (100g)
- 2 large eggs
- 1/2 cup sugar free eggnog (120ml)
- 1 teaspoon vanilla extract (5ml)
- 1/2 teaspoon ground nutmeg
- Whipped cream, for topping (optional)
- Ground nutmeg, for garnish (optional)

Instructions:

1. Preheat your oven to 325°F (160°C) and grease a 9inch springform pan.
2. In a mixing bowl, combine almond flour, powdered erythritol, and melted butter until a crumbly dough forms.
3. Press the dough evenly into the bottom of the prepared springform pan to form the crust.
4. In another mixing bowl, beat cream cheese and powdered erythritol until smooth and creamy.
5. Add eggs, one at a time, beating well after each addition.
6. Mix in sugarfree eggnog, vanilla extract, and ground nutmeg until smooth.
7. Pour the cheesecake batter over the prepared crust and smooth the top with a spatula.
8. Bake in the preheated oven for 4550 minutes, or until the edges are set but the center still jiggles slightly.
9. Turn off the oven and let the cheesecake cool in the oven with the door cracked open for 1 hour.
10. Remove the cheesecake from the oven and let it cool completely on a wire rack.
11. Once cooled, refrigerate the cheesecake for at least 4 hours, or until chilled and set.
12. Before serving, top the keto eggnog cheesecake with whipped cream and a sprinkle of ground nutmeg if desired.
13. Slice and enjoy this creamy and indulgent holiday dessert!

Nutritional Info (per serving): Calories: 280 | Fat: 25g | Carbs: 5g | Protein: 7g

SUGARFREE CRANBERRY ORANGE BREAD

Prep: 15 mins | Bake: 45 mins | Serves: 10

Ingredients:

- 2 cups almond flour (240g)
- 1/3 cup powdered erythritol (65g)
- 1 teaspoon baking powder (5g)
- 1/4 teaspoon salt
- Zest of 1 orange
- 1/3 cup unsweetened almond milk (80ml)
- 1/4 cup fresh orange juice (60ml)
- 2 large eggs
- 1/4 cup melted coconut oil (60ml)
- 1 teaspoon vanilla extract (5ml)
- 1/2 cup fresh or frozen cranberries (60g), chopped

Instructions:

1. Preheat your oven to 350°F (175°C) and grease a 9x5inch loaf pan.
2. In a large mixing bowl, whisk together almond flour, powdered erythritol, baking powder, salt, and orange zest.
3. In another mixing bowl, whisk together unsweetened almond milk, orange juice, eggs, melted coconut oil, and vanilla extract until well combined.
4. Pour the wet ingredients into the dry ingredients and mix until just combined.
5. Gently fold in chopped cranberries until evenly distributed throughout the batter.
6. Pour the batter into the prepared loaf pan and spread it out evenly.
7. Bake in the preheated oven for 4045 minutes, or until a toothpick inserted into the center comes out clean.
8. Remove the bread from the oven and let it cool in the pan for 10 minutes before transferring it to a wire rack to cool completely.
9. Once cooled, slice and serve this delicious sugarfree cranberry orange bread as a festive treat!

Nutritional Info (per serving): Calories: 190 | Fat: 16g | Carbs: 6g | Protein: 6g

Prep: 15 mins | Chill: 30 mins | Bake: 12 mins | Serves: 12

Ingredients:

- 1 cup almond flour (120g)
- 1/4 cup powdered erythritol (50g)
- 1/4 teaspoon vanilla extract (1.25ml)
- 1/4 cup unsalted butter, softened (60g)
- Pinch of salt

Instructions:

1. In a mixing bowl, combine almond flour, powdered erythritol, vanilla extract, softened butter, and a pinch of salt.
2. Mix the ingredients until a dough forms.
3. Shape the dough into a ball and wrap it in plastic wrap.
4. Chill the dough in the refrigerator for 30 minutes.
5. Preheat your oven to 350°F (175°C) and line a baking sheet with parchment paper.
6. Remove the chilled dough from the refrigerator and roll it out on a lightly floured surface to about 1/4inch thickness.
7. Use cookie cutters to cut out shapes from the dough and place them on the prepared baking sheet.
8. Bake in the preheated oven for 1012 minutes, or until the edges are lightly golden.
9. Remove from the oven and let the cookies cool on the baking sheet for a few minutes before transferring them to a wire rack to cool completely.
10. Once cooled, serve and enjoy these delightful lowcarb shortbread cookies!

Nutritional Info (per serving 2 cookies): Calories: 120 | Fat: 11g | Carbs: 3g | Protein: 3g

Prep: 15 mins | Chill: 1 hour | Serves: 12

Ingredients:

- 8 ounces sugarfree dark chocolate, chopped (225g)
- 1/2 cup sugarfree white chocolate chips (90g)
- 1/2 teaspoon peppermint extract (2.5ml)
- 2 tablespoons crushed sugarfree peppermint candies (optional)

Instructions:

1. Line a baking sheet with parchment paper.
2. In a heatproof bowl set over a pot of simmering water, melt the sugarfree dark chocolate, stirring until smooth.
3. Once melted, pour the melted dark chocolate onto the prepared baking sheet and spread it out evenly with a spatula.
4. Place the baking sheet in the refrigerator to chill for about 15 minutes, or until the chocolate has set.
5. In another heatproof bowl set over a pot of simmering water, melt the sugarfree white chocolate chips, stirring until smooth.
6. Remove from heat and stir in peppermint extract until well combined.
7. Pour the melted white chocolate over the chilled dark chocolate layer and spread it out evenly.
8. If desired, sprinkle crushed sugarfree peppermint candies over the white chocolate layer.
9. Return the baking sheet to the refrigerator and chill for another 3045 minutes, or until the bark is completely set.
10. Once set, break the keto peppermint bark into pieces and serve.
11. Store any leftovers in an airtight container in the refrigerator.

Nutritional Info (per serving): Calories: 120 | Fat: 10g | Carbs: 5g | Protein: 2g

Prep: 30 mins | Chill: 1 hour | Serves: 6

Ingredients:

- 6 ounces sugarfree dark chocolate, chopped (170g)
- 1/2 cup cocoa powder (unsweetened) (50g)
- 1/4 cup powdered erythritol (50g)
- 2 cups unsweetened almond milk (480ml)
- Sugarfree marshmallows, for filling (optional)

Instructions:

1. In a heatproof bowl set over a pot of simmering water, melt half of the sugarfree dark chocolate, stirring until smooth.
2. Using a spoon or a silicone brush, coat the insides of 6 halfsphere silicone molds with the melted chocolate.
3. Place the molds in the refrigerator to chill for about 10 minutes, or until the chocolate has set.
4. Remove the molds from the refrigerator and apply a second coat of melted chocolate to reinforce the shells. Return to the refrigerator to chill for another 10 minutes.
5. In a mixing bowl, whisk together cocoa powder and powdered erythritol.
6. Heat unsweetened almond milk in a saucepan over medium heat until warmed but not boiling.
7. Whisk the cocoa powder mixture into the warmed almond milk until well combined and smooth.
8. Remove the hot chocolate mixture from heat and let it cool slightly.
9. Spoon the hot chocolate mixture into the chilled chocolate shells, filling each about halfway.
10. If desired, add sugarfree marshmallows to the center of each bomb.
11. Melt the remaining sugarfree dark chocolate and use it to seal the filled chocolate shells by spreading it around the edges.
12. Return the molds to the refrigerator to chill for at least 1 hour, or until the hot chocolate bombs are completely set.
13. To serve, place a hot chocolate bomb in a mug and pour hot almond milk over it. Stir until the bomb has completely melted, and enjoy a delicious sugarfree hot chocolate!

Nutritional Info (per serving 1 hot chocolate bomb): Calories: 150 | Fat: 12g | Carbs: 7g | Protein: 3g

Prep: 20 mins | Bake: 1 hour | Serves: 12

Ingredients:

- 1 cup almond flour (120g)
- 1/4 cup coconut flour (30g)
- 1/4 cup powdered erythritol (50g)
- 1 teaspoon baking powder (5g)
- 1/2 teaspoon ground cinnamon
- 1/4 teaspoon ground nutmeg
- 1/4 teaspoon ground cloves
- 1/4 teaspoon salt
- 1/4 cup unsweetened applesauce (60ml)
- 1/4 cup melted coconut oil (60ml)
- 2 large eggs
- 1/2 cup chopped mixed nuts (60g)
- 1/2 cup chopped dried fruit (such as cranberries, apricots, and raisins) (80g)
- 1/4 cup rum or brandy (optional)

Instructions:

1. Preheat your oven to 350°F (175°C) and grease a loaf pan.
2. In a large mixing bowl, whisk together almond flour, coconut flour, powdered erythritol, baking powder, ground cinnamon, ground nutmeg, ground cloves, and salt.
3. In another mixing bowl, combine unsweetened applesauce, melted coconut oil, and eggs. Mix well.
4. Gradually add the wet ingredients to the dry ingredients and stir until just combined.
5. Fold in chopped mixed nuts and dried fruit. If using, soak the dried fruit in rum or brandy for added flavor.
6. Pour the batter into the prepared loaf pan and spread it out evenly.
7. Bake in the preheated oven for 5060 minutes, or until a toothpick inserted into the center comes out clean.
8. Remove from the oven and let the fruitcake cool in the pan for 10 minutes before transferring it to a wire rack to cool completely.
9. Once cooled, slice and serve this lowcarb fruitcake as a delicious holiday treat!

Nutritional Info (per serving): Calories: 180 | Fat: 14g | Carbs: 8g | Protein: 6g

Prep: 1 hour | Bake: 12 mins | Assemble: 1 hour | Serves: 68

Ingredients:

For the Gingerbread Dough:

- 3 cups almond flour (360g)
- 1/2 cup powdered erythritol (100g)
- 1 tablespoon ground ginger
- 1 tablespoon ground cinnamon
- 1/2 teaspoon ground cloves
- 1/2 teaspoon baking soda
- 1/4 teaspoon salt
- 1/4 cup unsalted butter, melted (60g)
- 1/4 cup sugarfree maple syrup (60ml)
- 1 large egg
- For the Royal Icing:
- 1 cup powdered erythritol (200g)
- 1 large egg white
- 1/2 teaspoon lemon juice

Instructions:

1. In a large mixing bowl, whisk together almond flour, powdered erythritol, ground ginger, ground cinnamon, ground cloves, baking soda, and salt.
2. In another mixing bowl, mix together melted unsalted butter, sugarfree maple syrup, and a large egg until well combined.
3. Gradually add the wet ingredients to the dry ingredients and mix until a dough forms.
4. Divide the dough into smaller portions and roll them out on a lightly floured surface to about 1/4inch thickness.
5. Use gingerbread house templates or cutters to cut out the shapes for the walls, roof, and other parts of the gingerbread house.
6. Place the cutout dough shapes on parchmentlined baking sheets and bake in a preheated oven at 350°F (175°C) for 1012 minutes, or until lightly golden.
7. While the gingerbread pieces are cooling, prepare the royal icing by whisking together powdered erythritol, egg white, and lemon juice until thick and smooth.
8. Once the gingerbread pieces are completely cooled, assemble the gingerbread house using the royal icing as the "glue".
9. Decorate the gingerbread house with additional royal icing and sugarfree candies or decorations as desired.
10. Let the assembled gingerbread house set for at least 1 hour before serving or displaying.

Nutritional Info (per serving): Calories: 280 | Fat: 24g | Carbs: 10g | Protein: 8g

Prep: 30 mins | Chill: 2 hours | Serves: 8

Ingredients:

- 1 batch Keto Pound Cake (cut into cubes)
- 2 cups sugarfree vanilla pudding
- 2 cups whipped cream
- 1 cup fresh berries (such as strawberries, blueberries, and raspberries)
- Sugarfree chocolate shavings, for garnish (optional)
- Fresh mint leaves, for garnish (optional)

Instructions:

1. Prepare a batch of keto pound cake and let it cool completely before cutting it into small cubes.
2. In a trifle dish or a large glass bowl, layer the bottom with half of the keto pound cake cubes.
3. Spoon half of the sugarfree vanilla pudding over the pound cake layer, spreading it out evenly.
4. Add half of the whipped cream on top of the pudding layer and spread it out.
5. Scatter half of the fresh berries over the whipped cream layer.
6. Repeat the layers with the remaining pound cake cubes, vanilla pudding, whipped cream, and fresh berries.
7. Cover the trifle dish with plastic wrap and refrigerate for at least 2 hours, or until chilled and set.
8. Before serving, garnish the sugarfree trifle with sugarfree chocolate shavings and fresh mint leaves if desired.
9. Serve chilled and enjoy this delightful sugarfree dessert!

Nutritional Info (per serving): Calories: 250 | Fat: 20g | Carbs: 10g | Protein: 5g

LOWCARB BÛCHE DE NOËL

Prep: 45 mins | Bake: 15 mins | Chill: 4 hours | Serves: 810

Ingredients:

For the Cake:

- 4 large eggs, separated
- 1/4 cup powdered erythritol (50g)
- 1/4 cup almond flour (30g)
- 2 tablespoons cocoa powder (unsweetened)
- 1/2 teaspoon vanilla extract (2.5ml)
- Pinch of salt

For the Filling:

- 1 cup heavy cream
- 2 tablespoons powdered erythritol (optional)
- 1 teaspoon vanilla extract (5ml)
- For the Chocolate Ganache:
- 4 ounces sugarfree dark chocolate, chopped (110g)
- 1/2 cup heavy cream
- 2 tablespoons powdered erythritol (optional)

Instructions:

1. Preheat your oven to 350°F (175°C) and line a 10x15inch baking sheet with parchment paper.
2. In a mixing bowl, beat egg yolks with powdered erythritol until pale and creamy.
3. Fold in almond flour, cocoa powder, vanilla extract, and a pinch of salt until well combined.
4. In a separate bowl, beat egg whites until stiff peaks form.
5. Gently fold the beaten egg whites into the chocolate mixture until fully incorporated.
6. Spread the batter evenly onto the prepared baking sheet and bake in the preheated oven for 1215 minutes, or until the cake is set and springs back when lightly touched.
7. While the cake is baking, prepare the filling by whipping heavy cream with powdered erythritol (if using) and vanilla extract until soft peaks form.
8. Once the cake is baked, let it cool in the pan for a few minutes, then carefully transfer it to a clean kitchen towel dusted with powdered erythritol.
9. Roll the cake up tightly with the towel and let it cool completely.
10. Carefully unroll the cake and spread the whipped cream filling evenly over the surface.
11. Roll the cake back up without the towel and place it seamside down on a serving platter.
12. To make the chocolate ganache, heat heavy cream in a saucepan until it begins to simmer.
13. Remove from heat and pour the hot cream over the chopped sugarfree dark chocolate. Let it sit for a minute, then whisk until smooth.
14. Let the ganache cool before pouring it over the rolled cake, allowing it to drip down the sides.
15. Refrigerate the Bûche de Noël for at least 4 hours, or until the ganache is set.
16. Before serving, decorate the cake with powdered erythritol, sugarfree chocolate shavings, or fresh berries if desired.
17. Slice and serve this festive lowcarb treat!

Nutritional Info (per serving): Calories: 220 | Fat: 18g | Carbs: 5g | Protein: 6g

Prep: 5 mins | Cook: 15 mins | Serves: 4

Ingredients:

- 1 bottle dry red wine (750ml)
- 1/4 cup powdered erythritol (50g)
- 1 orange, sliced
- 1 lemon, sliced
- 2 cinnamon sticks
- 4 whole cloves
- 2 star anise
- Optional garnish: orange or lemon slices, cinnamon sticks

Instructions:

1. In a saucepan, combine the dry red wine, powdered erythritol, sliced orange, sliced lemon, cinnamon sticks, cloves, and star anise.
2. Heat the mixture over mediumlow heat, stirring occasionally, until it reaches a gentle simmer.
3. Reduce the heat to low and let the mulled wine simmer for 1015 minutes to allow the flavors to meld together.
4. Taste the mulled wine and adjust sweetness, if needed, by adding more powdered erythritol.
5. Once ready, strain the mulled wine to remove the spices and citrus slices.
6. Pour the mulled wine into mugs or heatproof glasses.
7. Garnish each mug with a slice of orange or lemon and a cinnamon stick, if desired.
8. Serve the keto mulled wine warm and enjoy the cozy flavors of the holiday season!

Nutritional Info (per serving): Calories: 150 | Fat: 0g | Carbs: 5g | Protein: 0g

SUGARFREE CHRISTMAS PUDDING

Prep: 30 mins | Steam: 3 hours | Serves: 8

Ingredients:

- 1 cup almond flour (120g)
- 1/2 cup coconut flour (60g)
- 1/4 cup powdered erythritol (50g)
- 1/2 teaspoon baking powder (2.5g)
- 1/2 teaspoon ground cinnamon
- 1/4 teaspoon ground nutmeg
- 1/4 teaspoon ground cloves
- 1/4 teaspoon salt
- 1/4 cup unsweetened applesauce (60ml)
- 1/4 cup melted coconut oil (60ml)
- 2 large eggs
- 1/4 cup chopped mixed nuts (30g)
- 1/4 cup chopped dried fruit (such as cranberries, apricots, and raisins) (40g)
- 1/4 cup rum or brandy (optional)

Instructions:

1. In a large mixing bowl, whisk together almond flour, coconut flour, powdered erythritol, baking powder, ground cinnamon, ground nutmeg, ground cloves, and salt.
2. In another mixing bowl, mix together unsweetened applesauce, melted coconut oil, and eggs. Mix well.
3. Gradually add the wet ingredients to the dry ingredients and stir until just combined.
4. Fold in chopped mixed nuts and dried fruit. If using, soak the dried fruit in rum or brandy for added flavor.
5. Grease a heatproof pudding basin and line the base with parchment paper.
6. Spoon the pudding mixture into the basin and smooth the top with a spatula.
7. Cover the basin with a double layer of parchment paper and secure it with kitchen twine.
8. Place the basin in a large pot and pour boiling water into the pot until it reaches halfway up the sides of the basin.
9. Cover the pot with a lid and steam the pudding over low heat for 3 hours, topping up the water as needed.
10. Once steamed, remove the pudding from the pot and let it cool slightly before unmolding onto a serving plate.
11. Serve the sugarfree Christmas pudding warm, accompanied by sugarfree custard or whipped cream, if desired.
12. Enjoy the rich flavors of this festive dessert guiltfree!

Nutritional Info (per serving): Calories: 200 | Fat: 15g | Carbs: 8g | Protein: 6g

SUGARFREE CARAMEL SAUCE

Prep: 5 mins | Cook: 10 mins | Serves: 8

Ingredients:

- 1/2 cup erythritol (100g)
- 1/4 cup water (60ml)
- 1/4 cup heavy cream (60ml)
- 2 tablespoons unsalted butter (30g)
- 1 teaspoon vanilla extract (5ml)
- Pinch of salt

Instructions:

1. In a saucepan, combine erythritol and water over medium heat, stirring until erythritol is dissolved.
2. Let the mixture simmer without stirring until it turns a golden brown color, about 57 minutes.
3. Remove from heat and slowly whisk in heavy cream until smooth.
4. Add unsalted butter, vanilla extract, and a pinch of salt. Stir until the butter is melted and the sauce is well combined.
5. Let the caramel sauce cool slightly before serving.
6. Drizzle over your favorite desserts like ice cream or brownies.

Nutritional Info (per serving): Calories: 60 | Fat: 5g | Carbs: 2g | Protein: 0g

LOWCARB CHOCOLATE GANACHE

Prep: 5 mins | Cook: 5 mins | Serves: 8

Ingredients:

- 4 ounces sugarfree dark chocolate, chopped (110g)
- 1/2 cup heavy cream (120ml)
- 1 tablespoon powdered erythritol (optional)
- 1/2 teaspoon vanilla extract (2.5ml)

Instructions:

1. Place chopped sugarfree dark chocolate in a heatproof bowl.
2. In a saucepan, heat heavy cream over medium heat until it starts to simmer.
3. Pour the hot cream over the chopped chocolate and let it sit for 12 minutes.
4. Add powdered erythritol (if using) and vanilla extract to the bowl.
5. Whisk the mixture until smooth and glossy.
6. Let the ganache cool slightly before pouring it over cakes or desserts.

Nutritional Info (per serving): Calories: 80 | Fat: 7g | Carbs: 3g | Protein: 1g

KETO STRAWBERRY SAUCE

Prep: 5 mins | Cook: 10 mins | Serves: 8

Ingredients:

- 1 cup fresh strawberries, hulled and sliced (150g)
- 2 tablespoons powdered erythritol (optional)
- 1 tablespoon water (15ml)
- 1 teaspoon lemon juice (5ml)

Instructions:

1. In a saucepan, combine sliced strawberries, powdered erythritol (if using), water, and lemon juice.
2. Cook over medium heat, stirring occasionally, until the strawberries break down and the sauce thickens, about 810 minutes.
3. Remove from heat and let the sauce cool slightly.
4. Serve over pancakes, waffles, or ice cream.

Nutritional Info (per serving): Calories: 10 | Fat: 0g | Carbs: 3g | Protein: 0g

SUGARFREE LEMON CURD

Prep: 10 mins | Cook: 10 mins | Chill: 2 hours | Serves: 8

Ingredients:

- 3 large eggs
- 1/2 cup powdered erythritol (100g)
- Zest of 2 lemons
- 1/2 cup freshly squeezed lemon juice (120ml)
- 1/4 cup unsalted butter, cubed (60g)

Instructions:

1. In a heatproof bowl, whisk together eggs and powdered erythritol until smooth.
2. Stir in lemon zest and freshly squeezed lemon juice.
3. Place the bowl over a saucepan of simmering water (double boiler method).
4. Add cubed unsalted butter to the bowl and cook, stirring constantly, until the mixture thickens and coats the back of a spoon, about 810 minutes.
5. Remove from heat and let the lemon curd cool slightly.
6. Transfer the lemon curd to a jar or container and refrigerate for at least 2 hours, or until set.
7. Serve chilled with scones, muffins, or use as a filling for cakes and tarts.

Nutritional Info (per serving): Calories: 80 | Fat: 7g | Carbs: 2g | Protein: 2g

LOWCARB WHIPPED CREAM

Prep: 5 mins | Serves: 8

Ingredients:

- 1 cup heavy cream (240ml)
- 1 tablespoon powdered erythritol (optional)
- 1/2 teaspoon vanilla extract (2.5ml)

Instructions:

1. In a mixing bowl, combine heavy cream, powdered erythritol (if using), and vanilla extract.
2. Using a hand mixer or stand mixer, whip the cream on mediumhigh speed until stiff peaks form, about 23 minutes.
3. Be careful not to overmix, or the cream will become grainy.
4. Use immediately as a topping for desserts or store in the refrigerator until ready to use.

Nutritional Info (per serving): Calories: 100 | Fat: 10g | Carbs: 1g | Protein: 1g

KETO PEANUT BUTTER SAUCE

Prep: 5 mins | Cook: 5 mins | Serves: 8

Ingredients:

- 1/2 cup creamy peanut butter (120g)
- 1/4 cup coconut milk (60ml)
- 2 tablespoons powdered erythritol (optional)
- 1/2 teaspoon vanilla extract (2.5ml)
- Pinch of salt

Instructions:

1. In a small saucepan, combine creamy peanut butter, coconut milk, powdered erythritol (if using), vanilla extract, and a pinch of salt.
2. Heat the mixture over low heat, stirring continuously until smooth and well combined, about 35 minutes.
3. Remove from heat and let the peanut butter sauce cool slightly before serving.
4. Drizzle over pancakes, ice cream, or use as a dip for fruit slices.

Nutritional Info (per serving): Calories: 120 | Fat: 10g | Carbs: 4g | Protein: 4g

SUGARFREE RASPBERRY COULIS

Prep: 5 mins | Cook: 10 mins | Serves: 8

Ingredients:

- 1 cup fresh raspberries (150g)
- 2 tablespoons powdered erythritol (optional)
- 1 tablespoon water (15ml)
- 1 teaspoon lemon juice (5ml)

Instructions:

1. In a small saucepan, combine fresh raspberries, powdered erythritol (if using), water, and lemon juice.
2. Cook over medium heat, stirring occasionally, until the raspberries break down and the mixture thickens slightly, about 810 minutes.
3. Remove from heat and let the raspberry coulis cool slightly.
4. Transfer the mixture to a blender or use an immersion blender to puree until smooth.
5. Strain the coulis through a finemesh sieve to remove the seeds, if desired.
6. Serve the raspberry coulis drizzled over cheesecakes, pancakes, or desserts.

Nutritional Info (per serving): Calories: 10 | Fat: 0g | Carbs: 3g | Protein: 0g

LOWCARB BUTTERSCOTCH SAUCE

Prep: 5 mins | Cook: 10 mins | Serves: 8

Ingredients:

- 1/2 cup heavy cream (120ml)
- 1/4 cup unsalted butter (60g)
- 1/4 cup powdered erythritol (50g)
- 1 teaspoon vanilla extract (5ml)
- Pinch of salt

Instructions:

1. In a saucepan, combine heavy cream, unsalted butter, powdered erythritol, vanilla extract, and a pinch of salt.
2. Cook over medium heat, stirring constantly, until the mixture comes to a simmer.
3. Reduce the heat to low and continue to cook, stirring occasionally, until the sauce thickens and coats the back of a spoon, about 810 minutes.
4. Remove from heat and let the butterscotch sauce cool slightly before serving.
5. Drizzle over ice cream, cakes, or use as a dip for apple slices.

Nutritional Info (per serving): Calories: 120 | Fat: 12g | Carbs: 1g | Protein: 0g

KETO CREAM CHEESE FROSTING

Prep: 5 mins | Serves: 8

Ingredients:

- 4 ounces cream cheese, softened (110g)
- 1/4 cup powdered erythritol (50g)
- 1/4 cup heavy cream (60ml)
- 1/2 teaspoon vanilla extract (2.5ml)

Instructions:

1. In a mixing bowl, beat softened cream cheese and powdered erythritol until smooth and creamy.
2. Add heavy cream and vanilla extract to the bowl.
3. Continue to beat until the frosting is light and fluffy, about 23 minutes.
4. Use immediately to frost cakes, cupcakes, or cookies.
5. Store any leftovers in the refrigerator.

Nutritional Info (per serving): Calories: 90 | Fat: 9g | Carbs: 1g | Protein: 1g

SUGARFREE BLUEBERRY COMPOTE

Prep: 5 mins | Cook: 10 mins | Serves: 8

Ingredients:

- 1 cup fresh blueberries (150g)
- 2 tablespoons powdered erythritol (optional)
- 1 tablespoon water (15ml)
- 1 teaspoon lemon juice (5ml)
- 1/2 teaspoon vanilla extract (2.5ml)

Instructions:

1. In a saucepan, combine fresh blueberries, powdered erythritol (if using), water, lemon juice, and vanilla extract.
2. Cook over medium heat, stirring occasionally, until the blueberries burst and the mixture thickens slightly, about 810 minutes.
3. Remove from heat and let the blueberry compote cool slightly.
4. Serve warm or chilled over pancakes, waffles, or yogurt.

Nutritional Info (per serving): Calories: 10 | Fat: 0g | Carbs: 3g | Protein: 0g

LOWCARB MAPLE SYRUP

Prep: 5 mins | Cook: 10 mins | Serves: 8

Ingredients:

- 1/2 cup water (120ml)
- 1/2 cup powdered erythritol (100g)
- 1 teaspoon maple extract (5ml)

Instructions:

1. In a saucepan, combine water and powdered erythritol over medium heat, stirring until erythritol is dissolved.
2. Let the mixture simmer until it reduces by half, about 57 minutes.
3. Remove from heat and stir in maple extract.
4. Let the lowcarb maple syrup cool before serving.
5. Use as a topping for pancakes, waffles, or oatmeal.

Nutritional Info (per serving): Calories: 5 | Fat: 0g | Carbs: 2g | Protein: 0g

KETO CHOCOLATE AVOCADO MOUSSE

Prep: 10 mins | Chill: 1 hour | Serves: 4

Ingredients:

- 2 ripe avocados
- 1/4 cup unsweetened cocoa powder (25g)
- 1/4 cup powdered erythritol (50g)
- 1/4 cup coconut cream (60ml)
- 1 teaspoon vanilla extract (5ml)
- Pinch of salt

Instructions:

1. In a blender or food processor, combine ripe avocados, unsweetened cocoa powder, powdered erythritol, coconut cream, vanilla extract, and a pinch of salt.
2. Blend until smooth and creamy, scraping down the sides of the blender as needed.
3. Divide the mousse into serving cups and refrigerate for at least 1 hour, or until chilled and set.
4. Serve topped with whipped cream or fresh berries, if desired.

Nutritional Info (per serving): Calories: 180 | Fat: 15g | Carbs: 9g | Protein: 3g

SUGARFREE CUSTARD SAUCE

Prep: 5 mins | Cook: 10 mins | Serves: 8

Ingredients:

- 2 cups unsweetened almond milk (480ml)
- 4 large egg yolks
- 1/4 cup powdered erythritol (50g)
- 2 tablespoons cornstarch (UK: cornflour)
- 1 teaspoon vanilla extract (5ml)
- Pinch of salt

Instructions:

1. In a saucepan, heat unsweetened almond milk over medium heat until warm, but not boiling.
2. In a mixing bowl, whisk together egg yolks, powdered erythritol, cornstarch (cornflour), vanilla extract, and a pinch of salt until smooth.
3. Slowly pour the warm almond milk into the egg yolk mixture, whisking constantly to combine.
4. Return the mixture to the saucepan and cook over medium heat, stirring constantly, until the custard thickens and coats the back of a spoon, about 57 minutes.
5. Remove from heat and let the custard sauce cool slightly before serving.
6. Serve warm or chilled over cakes, pies, or fresh fruit.

Nutritional Info (per serving): Calories: 50 | Fat: 3.5g | Carbs: 2g | Protein: 2g

LOWCARB COCONUT CREAM

Prep: 5 mins | Chill: 2 hours | Serves:

Ingredients:

- 1 can (13.5 oz) fullfat coconut milk, chilled
- 1 tablespoon powdered erythritol (optional)
- 1/2 teaspoon vanilla extract (2.5ml)

Instructions:

1. Chill the can of fullfat coconut milk in the refrigerator overnight.
2. Open the can of coconut milk and scoop out the thick cream that has risen to the top, leaving behind the liquid.
3. Place the thick coconut cream in a mixing bowl. Add powdered erythritol (if using) and vanilla extract.
4. Using a hand mixer or stand mixer, whip the coconut cream until light and fluffy, about 23 minutes.
5. Transfer the coconut cream to a container and refrigerate for at least 2 hours before serving.
6. Serve chilled as a topping for desserts or fruit salads.

Nutritional Info (per serving): Calories: 90 | Fat: 9g | Carbs: 1g | Protein: 1g

KETO SALTED CARAMEL SAUCE

Prep: 5 mins | Cook: 10 mins | Serves: 8

Ingredients:

- 1/2 cup heavy cream (120ml)
- 1/4 cup unsalted butter (60g)
- 1/4 cup powdered erythritol (50g)
- 1 teaspoon vanilla extract (5ml)
- 1/2 teaspoon sea salt (or to taste)

Instructions:

1. In a saucepan, combine heavy cream, unsalted butter, powdered erythritol, vanilla extract, and sea salt.
2. Cook over medium heat, stirring constantly, until the mixture comes to a simmer.
3. Reduce the heat to low and continue to cook, stirring occasionally, until the sauce thickens and coats the back of a spoon, about 810 minutes.
4. Remove from heat and let the salted caramel sauce cool slightly before serving.
5. Drizzle over ice cream, cakes, or use as a dip for apple slices.

Nutritional Info (per serving): Calories: 120 | Fat: 12g | Carbs: 1g | Protein: 0g

Day	BREAKFAST	LUNCH	DINNER	DESSERT
1	Keto Chaffle Waffles	Grilled Chicken Salad	Baked Salmon with Veggies	Keto Brownies
2	Greek Yogurt Panna Cotta	Low-carb Wrap	Steak with Asparagus	Almond Flour Cookies
3	Low-carb Zucchini Bread	Turkey Sandwich (low-carb bread)	Grilled Shrimp	Coconut Flour Muffins
4	Keto Peanut Butter Cups	Chicken Caesar Salad	Beef Stir-fry	Sugar-free Cheesecake
5	Keto Avocado Brownies	Tuna Salad	Pork Chops with Green Beans	Low-carb Lemon Bars
6	Low-carb Pecan Pie	Spinach & Feta Salad	Grilled Tilapia	Keto Chocolate Mousse
7	Low-carb Pecan Pie Bars	Cobb Salad	Roast Chicken	Sugar-free Jello Parfaits
8	Keto Cream Puffs	Eggplant Parmesan	Baked Cod	Keto Chocolate Truffles
9	Keto Chocolate Cake	Greek Salad	Lemon Garlic Chicken	Almond Butter Fudge
10	Almond Flour Cookies	BLT Salad	Stuffed Peppers	Coconut Flour Bread
11	Low-carb Tiramisu	Avocado Chicken Salad	BBQ Ribs	Keto Lemon Bars
12	Keto Ice Cream	Quinoa Salad	Turkey Meatballs	Low-carb Macaroons
13	Sugar-free Pumpkin Pie	Veggie Wrap	Grilled Salmon	Keto Avocado Brownies
14	Low-carb Tiramisu	Chicken Caesar Salad	Pork Tenderloin	Sugar-free Chocolate Truffles
15	Sugar-free Flan	Greek Salad	Beef Kebabs	Low-carb Chocolate Chip Cookies
16	Keto Custard Tarts	Tuna Salad	Chicken Fajitas	Sugar-free Hot Chocolate
17	Keto Cheesecake Bars	Caprese Salad	Grilled Steak	Low-carb Chocolate Brownies
18	Keto Chocolate Mousse Cups	Chicken Salad	Baked Cod	Low-carb Chocolate Tart
19	Chia Seed Pudding	Spinach & Bacon Salad	Roast Turkey	Keto Chocolate Lava Cakes
20	Keto Cannoli	Caesar Salad	Baked Salmon	Low-carb Chocolate Biscotti
21	Low-carb Crème Brûlée	Avocado Salad	BBQ Chicken	Sugar-free Chocolate Fondue

Day	BREAKFAST	LUNCH	DINNER	DESSERT
22	Sugar-free Pumpkin Pie	Egg Salad	Grilled Shrimp	Low-carb Chocolate Hazelnut Cookies
23	Greek Yogurt Panna Cotta	Turkey Wrap	Grilled Chicken	Keto Ice Cream Sandwiches
24	Keto Custard Tarts	Veggie Salad	Pork Chops	Low-carb Sorbet
25	Low-carb Tiramisu	Greek Salad	Steak with Mushrooms	Sugar-free Frosty
26	Sugar-free Cheesecake Bites	Chicken Caesar Salad	Baked Tilapia	Keto Peanut Butter Cups
27	Sugar-free Rice Pudding	Spinach Salad	Grilled Salmon	Keto Cream Puffs
28	Low-carb Crème Brûlée	Tuna Salad	Pork Tenderloin	Keto Chocolate Mousse
29	Keto Chocolate Cake	BLT Salad	Roast Chicken	Sugar-free Jello Parfaits
30	Sugar-free Pumpkin Pie	Greek Salad	Beef Stir-fry	Keto Chocolate Truffles

This plan can be adjusted based on individual preferences and dietary needs. Each dessert is taken from the respective chapters to provide a variety of flavors and textures.

As we reach the end of this delicious journey through diabetic friendly desserts, I hope you feel empowered and inspired to take control of your diet without sacrificing the sweet indulgences that bring you joy. Living with diabetes is a lifelong endeavor, but it doesn't have to be a life sentence devoid of flavor and satisfaction.

Throughout the pages of this cookbook, we've explored a world of possibilities – rich and decadent treats that not only satisfy your cravings but also nourish your body. We've discovered the joys of baking with alternative flours, natural sweeteners, and nutrient dense ingredients that transform seemingly forbidden desserts into guilt free pleasures.

From the fudgy depths of keto brownies and the creamy indulgence of sugarfree cheesecakes to the refreshing burst of fruitbased delights and the nutty crunch of seedy treats, we've proven that living with diabetes doesn't mean depriving yourself of the flavors and textures you love. It's about finding balance, making smart swaps, and embracing a mindset of moderation and self care.

As someone who has walked this path myself, I know firsthand the challenges and temptations that come with managing diabetes. There have been moments when the allure of a traditional, sugarladen dessert felt almost irresistible, threatening to derail my hardearned progress. But it was in those moments that I learned to lean on the recipes and strategies within these pages, discovering that true satisfaction can be found in desserts that nourish both my body and my soul.

I vividly remember the first time I sank my teeth into a perfectly fudgy keto brownie, the rich chocolate flavor melting on my tongue without a shred of guilt or worry about blood sugar spikes. It was a revelation – a reminder that desserts could still be an integral part of my life, just with a few tweaks and a whole lot of deliciousness.

And that's the true beauty of this cookbook – it's not about deprivation or settling for subpar imitations. It's about celebrating the art of baking and the joy of indulgence, while also prioritizing your health and wellbeing. Each recipe is a testament to the power of creativity, ingenuity, and a refusal to compromise on flavor.

As you flip through these pages, you'll find desserts for every occasion and craving imaginable. From decadent holiday treats that will make your celebrations feel extra special to refreshing frozen delights perfect for beating the summer heat, there's something to satisfy every sweet tooth. And with options for those following a gluten free, vegan, or lowcarb lifestyle, no one is left out of the fun.

But beyond the recipes themselves, this cookbook is also a celebration of community and shared experiences. As someone living with diabetes, I know the power of having a supportive network of friends, family, and fellow dessert enthusiasts who understand the unique challenges and triumphs that come with this journey.

Throughout the creation of this book, I've been humbled and inspired by the stories, tips, and recipes shared by others navigating the world of diabetic friendly baking. From the grandmother who perfected her sugar free pie recipe to the young baker who discovered the joys of almond flour, each contribution has added depth and richness to this collection.

In these pages, you'll find not just recipes but also a tapestry of personal anecdotes, hardwon wisdom, and heartfelt encouragement. Because at the end of the day, living with diabetes is about so much more than just the food we eat – it's about finding joy, connection, and self acceptance in even the smallest of moments.

As you embark on your own journey through these recipes, I encourage you to approach each one with an open mind and a willingness to explore new flavors and techniques. Embrace the process of experimentation, for it is in those moments of trial and error that true mastery is born.

Don't be afraid to tweak and adapt recipes to suit your personal preferences and dietary needs. Swap out ingredients, play with different sweeteners, and let your creativity run wild. Because at the heart of every successful dessert lies a spirit of fearless innovation and a refusal to be confined by limitations. And remember, desserts are meant to be savored and enjoyed, not just consumed out of habit or deprivation. So take the time to appreciate each bite, to revel in the textures and flavors that dance across your tongue. Share these treats with loved ones, and let them be a source of joy and connection, a reminder that even in the face of challenges, there is always room for sweetness in life.

As the pages of this cookbook come to a close, I leave you with a simple yet profound truth: desserts are not mere indulgences; they are expressions of love, creativity, and selfcare. They are reminders that even in the midst of managing a condition like diabetes, there is always room for pleasure, for celebration, and for savoring the sweet moments that make life truly worth living.

So go forth, my fellow dessert enthusiasts, and embrace the delicious possibilities that lie ahead. Let this cookbook be your guide, your inspiration, and your constant companion on a journey towards sweet satisfaction and balanced living. For in the end, it's not just about the desserts we create, but the memories, connections, and moments of pure delight that they inspire.

Printed in Great Britain
by Amazon

44282019R00084